FRENCH-SPEAKING WEST AFRICA

FRENCH-SPEAKING WEST AFRICA

From Colonial Status to Independence

PHILIP NERES

C'est la juste délimitation entre
le recours à la force et le refus
d'imposer qui est, en politique,
la vraie modération.
          Jean Lacouture, 1961

*Issued under the auspices of the
Institute of Race Relations, London*

OXFORD UNIVERSITY PRESS

LONDON   NEW YORK

1962

Oxford University Press, Amen House, London E.C.4

GLASGOW NEW YORK TORONTO MELBOURNE WELLINGTON
BOMBAY CALCUTTA MADRAS KARACHI LAHORE DACCA
CAPE TOWN SALISBURY NAIROBI IBADAN ACCRA
KUALA LUMPUR HONG KONG

Printed in Great Britain

TO
MY MOTHER

CONTENTS

INTRODUCTION

ELSPETH Huxley is reported to have written a letter, in 1959, in which she said that 'trying to write a book about Africa nowadays is like attempting to photograph a horse race with an ancient camera: the subject is moving so fast that you are lucky if your film shows more than a blurred shape'.[1]

This erratic vision is certainly all that is vouchsafed to anyone who studies the independent West African states formerly under French rule. These states are Senegal, Mauritania, Mali (known as Soudan until 1959), Niger, Guinea, the Ivory Coast, Dahomey, Upper Volta and Togo. And in them, as Smith Hempstone has pointed out, 'is taking place the great experiment of African freedom'.[2]

With the exception of Togo—at first a German protectorate, then from 1922 a French mandate governed under the terms of the League of Nations agreements, and from 1946 to 1959 a United Nations Trust Territory administered by France—all these states were from 1904 to 1959 local units of the federation known as 'l'Afrique Occidentale Française' (A.O.F.). They were termed 'colonies' under the Third Republic[3] and 'overseas territories' under the Fourth. By means of the referendum on the Fifth Republic's proposed constitution, in September 1958, these territories opted—with the exception of Guinea which voted for total independence—for membership of the French Community and were declared to be 'Autonomous Republics'.

In December 1958, Senegal, Soudan, Upper Volta and Dahomey agreed to form the federal state of Mali. A federal constitution was drawn up in Dakar in January

[1] Smith Hempstone, *The New Africa* (London, Faber, 1961.) pp. 644–645.
[2] Ibid., p. 14.
[3] Upper Volta did not exist as a separate unit between 1932 and 1947. During those years it was partitioned between the Ivory Coast, Niger and Soudan.

1959, but within thirty days of the election of Modibo Keita of Soudan as President of Mali, Félix Houphouët-Boigny of the Ivory Coast detached two of the four states from the federation. As the price for secession from Mali, Houphouët-Boigny was forced to agree to the creation of the 'Conseil de l'Entente' constituted by the Ivory Coast, Upper Volta, Niger and Dahomey. The two remaining members of the Federation of Mali split in August 1960; Senegal retained its original name, but Soudan took over the name of the disbanded Federation and later joined the Ghana-Guinea Union.

Between April and November 1960, the West African 'Autonomous Republics' formerly in the A.O.F. successively acquired their independence. As a result, their relations with France are those of sovereign states. With the exception of the Republics of Mali and Togo all the West African republics have signed treaties or agreements of co-operation with France. Senegal is the only West African republic sharing special treaty obligations with France that has reaffirmed its membership of the French Community. The other republics have declined to do so.

No other continent displays quite as definitely as Africa the imprint of purely physical factors upon the social, political and economic development of its peoples. Varying external political forces and methods have had very considerable influence, for at least two millennia, on Africa. In West Africa the contrasting aims and results of French, British, Portuguese, Spanish and, more recently, Liberian policies, in their turn and side by side, succeeded the objectives and methods of Berbers, Arabs and Jews, which had previously been superimposed—except in the rain forest regions along the coast—upon the aboriginal African patterns of life. The latter were usually primitive, though here and there tribal groups coalesced into states whose political, and more particularly artistic, achievements proved not inconsiderable.

But in the second half of the twentieth century Africa has acquired a very special significance for, as *The Times* stated in its third leader on 1 December 1949:

Africa is the new continent; she is a focus of twentieth-century development, the centre of special problems of race, and the link between Europe and the Americas, on one side; and between Europe and Australia, New Zealand and the Far East on the other. The importance of Africa is seen in Moscow as well as in London and Washington.

Writing in 1962, one must add Paris and Peking to the three capitals mentioned by *The Times*. For whereas in 1949 France's Governments were struggling hopelessly against fearful odds in a war waged in Indo-China by Hô Chi Minh and the Viet-Minh which dragged on until 1954, the more recent war in Algeria and the sagacity of General de Gaulle have combined to focus the French nation's attention on *African* problems. The intensity of this attention, so far as colonial matters are concerned, can only have been equalled by that generated during the spacious days of colonial ambition associated with Jules Ferry's tenure of office. Similarly, in 1949, China was in no position, either internally or in its potential capacity as a world power, to affect conditions and developments in Africa. But today, under the leadership of Chou En-lai, China has discovered in Africa a valuable counter-irritant to its exclusion from the comity of the United Nations. This is achieved by activities injurious to the interests of the West in various areas of Africa. The most propitious of these for the Chinese remains Guinea whose President, a professed Muslim, is a Marxist who spent some time in 1947 in Czechoslovakia, in what has been described as an 'école de cadres'.[4]

A close watch on French-speaking West Africa is also now being kept from Cairo by both President Nasser and the Afro-Asian People's Solidarity Permanent Organisation, which has elected to establish its headquarters in the

[4] Jean Lacouture, *Cinq hommes et la France* (Paris, Editions du Seuil, 1961) p. 329.

capital of the United Arab Republic. About 48 per cent of the population of the former A.O.F. federation are Muslims[5], many of whom are easy prey to Arab nationalist propaganda. Yet the majority of West Africans are animists at heart, and animistic beliefs underlie the professed Islamic creed of the Muslims—whether Touareg or Ouolof, even though the latter are considered to be the most 'évolué' people of French West Africa—just as animistic beliefs underlie the orthodoxy of the majority of West African Christians. Local religious leaders, some of whom use their influence in an unscrupulous manner, thus have an important role to play in the formation and crystallisation of beliefs and ritual. Religious fanaticism has become another weapon in the hands of exiled African leaders (of whom there are many from the French-speaking territories) or of their sponsors.

Both the United Arab Republic and Morocco have been encouraging the spread of Islam in Senegal and spend considerable sums of money which, it is reasonable to suppose, they can ill-afford, in an endeavour to convince the simpler folk that their country should be headed by a Muslim and not by Léopold Sédar Senghor, a Christian with a French wife. It has been said that Nasser's agents spent £58,000, during 1960, in Senegal alone. With its Christian President and Muslim Prime Minister, Senegal could well become a fissile society and an easy target for the unscrupulous. The impact of Islam is always far more complex than any listing of historical and psychological factors might suggest.

The new forces at work since 1945 from Guinea to Niger are revolutionary. For, although French possessions in Africa were swept into the stream of world activity, by the turn of the century regionalism and religion, together with the powerfully disruptive character of France's colonial

[5] J. Spencer Trimingham, *Islam in West Africa*, (London, Oxford University Press, 1959), appendix V, p. 233.

policy—an amalgam of direct administration and assimilation—were sufficient, until 1945, to retard the development
of nationalism in French West Africa.

But nationalism has now replaced the mild feeling of
racialism which used to characterise the contact between
Africans and Frenchmen and other Europeans, whether in
Abidjan or on the Left Bank, in the trenches in France
during the First World War or in Senegal's Ecole Normale
William-Ponty, described as the 'nerve centre, the most
solid link which joined the élite'[6] of French West Africa.

At the same time, and to an extent that is perhaps
difficult to realise under conditions of great change (such
as the emergence of an urban proletariat, the cultivation of
cash crops and the development of mining), certain
traditional ideas, institutions and psychological attitudes are
preserved. The new communities, with a new pattern of
communal life unevenly superimposed upon the old, still
draw vitality from their ancient roots. Principles of
independence and personal responsibility, however wide-
spread their acceptance has become, have by no means
altogether replaced the basic conception of African community life. The past still lives on to a degree that has not
been experienced in Western Europe since the days of the
uneven and difficult transition from the medieval polity to
the nation-state. Thus the pace at which Africans in
French-speaking West Africa have recently been called on
to make several far-reaching political decisions—foremost
amongst which has been that on the nature of the relationship with France—must partly account for the fact that the
problem of the political relations among the African
territories themselves has not by any means been con-
clusively settled.

[6] *Genèse*, Ponty Alumni Association bulletin, April 1945, quoted by
Thomas Hodgkin and Ruth Schachter in *French-speaking West Africa in
Transition* (New York, International Conciliation, No. 528, May 1960)
p. 385.

It is true, of course, that the conferences of Abidjan and Brazzaville (in October and December 1960, attended by representatives from the countries in black Africa once ruled by France, except Guinea, Mali, Togo and Madagascar) and that of Yaoundé (which took place in March 1961, with the additional participation of Madagascar) have paved the way for a certain degree of political co-operation and co-ordination between the members of the 'Union Africaine et Malgache' (U.A.M.), founded at Yaoundé. Only six African countries now remain in the French Community: Senegal, Madagascar, Gabon, Congo, Tchad and the République Centrafricaine. But it would be a mistake to attach too much importance to the possible advantages of Community membership and M. Dia, the Prime Minister of Senegal, was right when he said: 'The fact of being or not being in the Community is an outdated verbal quarrel. Co-operation between the states . . . dominates the question of agreeing or not agreeing on the idea of Community.'[7]

The trend has been quite definitely against the creation of primary federations. Whereas the Union of Sahel-Bénin, which set up the 'Conseil de l'Entente', and the Ghana-Guinea-Mali Union are loose associations, all attempts at establishing a form of closer union have failed, very largely because of the opposition of M. Houphouët-Boigny to the rebirth of federal government in French-speaking West Africa. The mystique that has inspired M. Houphouët-Boigny—his belief that Frenchmen and Africans could create a new dimension in racial and international co-operation—is not unlike that which informs the policies of President de Gaulle, of whom he is a devoted admirer. This explains the Ivory Coast leader's firm adherence to the French Community until 1960 and his reluctance to see his country enter a federation with other states of West Africa.

[7] The Economist Intelligence Unit's Three-Monthly Economic Review of *French African Community, Togo, Cameroun, Guinea and Liberia*, no. 5 May 1961, p. 1.

These factors are fundamental to the understanding of the direction of political developments in contemporary French-speaking West Africa, where political choice is just as much conditioned as it is elsewhere by economic factors. Indeed, these account even more than certain political incompatibilities for the fact that, so far, political re-integration has not taken place.

In an address which he gave at Chatham House on 7 June 1961, President Modibo Keita of Mali stated:

Our constitution therefore provides for a total or partial abandonment of sovereignty in favour of a grouping of African States, but such an abandonment of sovereignty demands an identity of views with our fellow-States. One cannot build a whole with contradictions. Certain common viewpoints on international policy and on economic policy are absolutely necessary, together with an understanding of the contradictions contained in economic planning, and the necessity for each State to consider its economy within the framework of one large African economy, if it is to constitute an entity with the other States. For this reason we recognize that this abandonment of sovereignty necessitates an identity of views with our partners, both in foreign and domestic policy[8].

Thus, although a political and economic 'New Deal' for French Africa followed in the wake of the Second World War and although the economy of the A.O.F. itself expanded at a rate unparalleled during its previous history, the obvious lack of economic cohesion, and the markedly unequal geographical distribution of income gave rise to grave problems of federal finance. These contributed very considerably to the breaking up of the federation which had lasted since 1904, and have so far frustrated all attempts at rebuilding it.

---

[8] *International Affairs* (Oxford University Press, issued under the auspices of the Royal Institute of International Affairs), vol. 37, no. 4, October 1961, pp. 435–436.

French West Africa, 1904–59

LIBYA

FRENCH EQUATORIAL AFRICA

Abéché

Fort Archambault

Fort Lamy

Lake Tchad

ALGERIA

Ghat

AHAGGAR

Tamanrasset

Niger

Agadès

Zinder

Kano

CAMEROUN FR. MANDATE

CAMEROONS BR. MANDATE

Yaoundé

Douala

FRENCH WEST AFRICA

Benue

NIGERIA

Ibadan

Lagos

Porto Novo

Niger

Niamey

Soudan

DAHOMEY

TOGO FR. MAND.

BR. MAND.

Lome

Accra

Timbouctou

Ouagadougou

Volta

Upper Volta

Niger

Volta

GOLD COAST

Okumasi

Takoradi

S A H A R A

RIO DE ORO

Mauritania

SENEGAL

Port Etienne

Nouakchott

St. Louis

Dakar

Senegal

GAMBIA

Bathurst

PORT. GUINEA

FR. GUINEA

Bamako

Niger

IVORY COAST

Abidjan

LIBERIA

SIERRA LEONE

Conakry

Freetown

Monrovia

MILES

0 100 200 300

© SGE EDWARD STANFORD LTD, LONDON.

I HISTORY

IN 1405 a Frenchman, Anselme d'Isalguier of Toulouse, reached Gao on the Niger.[1] But it was the Portuguese who first fully explored the coast itself. The Senegal River was discovered in 1445 and some of its people had already become converts to Islam when the Italian, Cadamosto, visited them in 1453. Prince Henry the Navigator sent a mission to the Gambia in 1458, to convert Africans to Christianity, and by 1480 the whole of the Guinea coast was known to the Portuguese, who established numerous forts and trading-posts and began to trade for alluvial gold.

The Arabs from North Africa have from the eleventh century on engaged in profitable trade with the successive empires of the middle Niger, to which they introduced European goods. But the trade of greatest significance for the future, and the most lucrative, was that in slaves: for over a thousand years Arabs led African slaves across the Sahara to North Africa, Portugal and Spain or from the east coast of Africa to Asia.

Better protected owing to their geographical isolation, the Mossi kingdoms of Yatenga and Ouagadougou to the east, preferred the gentler agricultural and commercial pursuits and eschewed wars of conquest. As a result, they remained virtually intact until the penetration of the region of the upper Volta by the French in the nineteenth century.

The Sudanese empires and centralised states included hardly any of the forest lands of the southern region of West Africa, for cavalry—upon which the military supremacy of the Sudanese rulers rested—was ineffective in the forests, where ambushes proved as deadly as the tsetse fly. Hausa- and Mande-speaking Dioula merchants, however, in quest of the gold, ivory, slaves, peppers and

[1] C. de la Roncière, *La découverte de l'Afrique au moyen age* (Cairo, Société Royale de Géographie d'Egypte, 1924–27) vol. 3, pp. 1–6.

cola-nuts which entered into the trans-Saharan traffic, penetrated into the forest, whose peoples became influenced by Sudanese institutions. Forest kingdoms of considerable power, such as that of Benin, were already established at the time of the first Portuguese landing in the Bight of Benin (by Ruy de Siqueira in 1472). By the turn of the eighteenth century two other powerful states had emerged: the Ashanti confederation and the kingdom of Dahomey.

The European connexion, with its attendant supply of firearms in quantities unprecedented in Africa, followed by the gradual substitution of Atlantic for Saharan trade routes, slowly altered the balance of forces between savannah and forest, between Muslim and pagan; the ceremonial and state organisation of Ashanti and Dahomey came to bear a close resemblance to those of the displaced empires of Ghana, Mali and Gao.

Until the fifteenth century, West Africa's only contact with the outside world had been indirect, through the intermediary of traders and invaders from North Africa. But from the time that Europeans developed trading and political connexions in West Africa the consequences of direct contact with the outside world were momentous. The empires of the disintegrating western Sudan were completely surpassed in both wealth and importance by the forest states near the sea, and the provision of slaves rapidly became the foremost activity of African society. By 1455 over 700 slaves were imported into Portugal, and in the following century the value of the trade in African slaves, as in gold, ivory and spices, was such as to encourage English mariners, as well as Spaniards, Frenchmen, Dutchmen and Danes, to busy themselves with an area yielding so great a profit.

The object of their enterprises was to obtain trade rather than to found outposts of empire, and little interest was then shown in the interior. In the seventeenth century Portugal's supremacy in West Africa passed to Holland and in the eighteenth and nineteenth centuries to England and

France. During these centuries many millions of people were sold into slavery or were brutally captured. They were transported across the Atlantic to provide a helpless labour force for the European plantations. It is one of the quirks of history that the slave trade initiated by Portugal produced two of the main sources of West African wealth in the twentieth century. Ground-nuts were first introduced to West Africa from America by the Portuguese—probably to serve as food for slaves on the voyage across the Atlantic. Cocoa also was imported by the Portuguese into San Thomé and from there, as well as from the Spanish possession of Fernando Po, was introduced into the Gold Coast, where its large-scale cultivation in recent times has been the source of great wealth.[2]

At the same time, the consequences of the spread of Islam throughout Africa from the earliest days of Arab penetration of sub-Saharan Africa have been profound. The Arabic language and script were taught and used as the necessary vehicle of an educational system based on the teachings of the Koran and the study of the sciences; centres of learning were developed at Jenne and Timbuctu, whilst contacts were fostered between the Western Sudan and the great religious and cultural centres of the Arab world. Islam's influence on political organisation and the strengthening of dynastic control came to be considerable. Being a social as well as a religious system, it introduced new standards of conduct and of dress. By its insistence on sobriety and cleanliness, and by its exclusion of practices such as cannibalism and blood revenge, it raised numerous tribes to a level of civilisation hitherto unknown to them. It also helped to weld the existing congeries of tribal groups into larger entities. But it was a system based on slavery.

Towards the end of the eighteenth century, with the increasing realisation in Europe of the horrors of the slave

---

[2] In 1898, the Gold Coast exported 188 metric tons of cocoa beans; in 1918, 67,404 metric tons; in 1938, 261,557 metric tons; and in 1957, 264,400 metric tons.

trade, keen interest was aroused in the hinterland regions of Africa, which constituted the main source of the supply of slaves. The unsynchronised abolition of slavery by the European powers (France carried this out as late as 1848 and only as a result of the liberal upsurge accompanying the February Revolution), together with the need to obtain new sources of raw materials, provided impetus for the penetration of the interior. Governments in Europe were gradually prompted to envisage the possibility of acquiring territorial possession or, at the very least, political rights.

Senegal constituted the colonial nucleus from which French expansion throughout West Africa developed in the second half of the nineteenth century. The French had been on the African coast a long time before then. There had been a permanent French settlement (the extent of whose boundaries varied in accordance with the vicissitudes of the Anglo-French colonial struggle throughout the eighteenth century and up to 1815) since 1659, the date of the foundation of Saint-Louis. The fort and trading-post of Saint-Louis du Sénégal, which submitted its own 'cahier' for the Estates-General of 1789, together with the small island of Gorée captured from the Dutch in 1677, came to be the focal point of French power on the West African coast. It was used energetically by Faidherbe, whom Napoleon III sent there in 1854, as a base from which to transform, within the space of ten years, a cordon of stagnant and isolated trading-posts into a large territory, adding a hinterland to the coastal dependencies. This hinterland of desert and scrub, which Joost van Vollenhoven, one of France's most brilliant colonial administrators, described as a 'lunar landscape', was intended to provide both a balance for the hitherto coastal colony and a jumping-off ground for France's share in the 'scramble for Africa'. In order to accomplish this, Faidherbe astutely established relations with the local chiefs, drove back the Moors and Tou-couleurs, and opened up the whole of the territory later known as Senegal to trade, thereby clearing a way to the richer and more populous Niger Basin which various British expeditions were trying to reach from the sea.

During the same period, isolated posts were established between Grand Bassam and Porto Novo, thus providing effective 'points d'appui' on the Ivory Coast and in Dahomey for systematic expansion inland. The explorers Caillé, Magé and Binger emphasised that such northward expansion would provide the geographical unity lacking in possessions which were isolated along the coast of the Gulf of Guinea and scattered between British zones of occupation or influence, such as Sierra Leone and the Gold Coast. By 1870, France had created a compact territory in Senegal as far inland as Medina. After Faidherbe's departure from the colony in 1865, however, the French made virtually no advance in West Africa for about fifteen years.

The motives behind France's rapid acquisition of extensive new colonies in Africa were as complex as those prompting all such ventures. They included, of course, the desire of some French industrialists and traders to draw upon new sources of vegetable oils, timber and rubber as well as that of others to increase their sales of cheap cotton goods. On the eve of the 'scramble for Africa', free trade ensured access to the raw materials overseas which had become essential to European traders at home. Furthermore, exports to overseas markets were very much smaller in volume than imports into Europe from these areas. The protectionist policies developed in the last quarter of the nineteenth century and after—based on the mistaken fear felt by European manufacturers that, as a result of the state of free competition which prevailed, there might soon be insufficient outlets for their goods—in practice led the industrialised countries of Europe and later the United States to increase their exports very considerably between 1875 and 1914. Yet only a minor percentage of this increase can be accounted for by exports to the newly acquired colonies of Africa, whose population was far too poor to be able to absorb new products on any appreciable scale.

Missionaries had an obvious and influential interest in the opening-up of the interior of the African continent. But even more important, because of its psychological impact on political leaders such as Freycinet and Ferry, was Napoleon III's humiliating defeat at Sedan and its cause and effect relationship to the resumption of intense colonial activity. The mainspring of French expansion was undoubtedly the febrile nationalism which developed in the wake of Sedan and which had not yet spent itself at the time of General Boulanger's political fiasco in 1889. France which, since 1815, had considered colonialism an essential ingredient in its political prestige, especially in relation to England, proved very much more touchy about such matters after Napoleon III's downfall. France therefore displayed unwillingness to tolerate Leopold II's interest in some of the areas bordering the Congo River or to countenance Italy's ambitions in Tunisia.

This aggressive attitude led the British to give more support to their missionaries and traders who, since the turn of the nineteenth century, had been active in African territories. Yet traders long continued to follow the best markets, not their respective flags, for there were many Europeans of different nationalities who had common economic interests in their dealings with Africans.

Advancing along the Senegal River and across to the Niger, the French came up against the agents of other powers, but especially those of Britain. The latter had as their goal the domination of the great emirates of what is now Nigeria. Not until 1898 were the various boundary disputes, some of which involved the Royal Niger Company, settled between the French and British. By then, however, France had won a new empire—rich, even if, as Lord Salisbury deprecatingly remarked at the time, a great deal of the territory was 'what agriculturalists would call very light land', only partly developed.

The value of the trade shipped from its coast and the obvious wealth of the Guinea interior had led to the occupation of the Guinea colony and to the occupation of the holy city of Timbo in 1881. In the same year, a military command for the upper Senegal was created at Kayes, the head of water transport on the Senegal. With the Senegal and Guinea bases secured in the rear, an advance up the Niger Basin took place in 1883, and Bamako was occupied. By 1891, Ségou (Soudan) was reached and a rapid advance developed to Timbuctu and beyond two years later. A feeble footing established on the Ivory Coast in 1883; the penetration of the narrow Dahomey hinterland, after the occupation of Cotonou in 1890; Binger's exploration of the region to be known as Upper Volta and the Foureau-Lamy expedition into the area now called Niger; all of these helped to make France the second greatest colonial empire in the world by 1900.

Within the space of twenty years, a handful of French officers, whose troops were almost wholly African, set France the task of creating a new civilisation in West Africa which, at the turn of the twentieth century, proved to be under-populated as a result of war, the slave-trade and disease. Dreams of compensating for superior German manpower with the aid of African troops were soon dispelled. Not all French officers shared the young Mangin's high opinion of African soldiers. For although the Senegalese, formed by Faidherbe into units—the famous 'tirailleurs'—in 1857, had proved themselves admirable fighters, the Africans of the more tropical colonies remained poor military material.

As early as the late eighties, Eugène Etienne, born in Algeria and a leader of the Colonial Party in the French Parliament, who had become Under-Secretary of State for the Colonies, adumbrated a plan for a union of Senegal and Dahomey reaching, through Timbuktu, into southern Algeria. Etienne was eagerly supported by the 'Comité de l'Afrique Française' formed in 1890 by 'un certain nombre de personnes animées d'un zèle patriotique' with the object of developing 'l'influence et le commerce français dans l'Afrique de l'ouest, du centre et du nord'.[3] The driving force behind the 'Comité' was a political journalist named Hyppolite Percher, who was a regular contributor to the *Journal des Débats* and (under the pseudonym Harry Alis) the author of books such as *A la conquête du Tchad* and *Nos africains*, which were very popular with the younger generation of his day. He became the General Secretary of the 'Comité' and the editor of its Bulletin, but was killed in a duel in 1895.

In August 1893, leading French industrialists, merchants and bankers constituted 'un syndicat des principales maisons françaises ayant des intérêts dans nos colonies' under the title 'L'Union Coloniale Française'. One of their principal aims was to encourage emigration to the colonies, despite the fact that France had no real need of 'colonies de peuplement'.[4] Subject to pressure from many sides, and as a result of conflicts of authority between French administrators on the spot, the French Government agreed to confer administrative unity on France's West African possessions, as it had done to Indo-China. A Governor-General was appointed in 1895, with the stipulation that the post should always be granted to a civilian. Four years later, French West Africa was organised into a 'fédération de colonies'. The Governor-General was to exercise authority over the five colonies: Senegal, Guinea, Upper-Senegal-Niger, Ivory Coast and Dahomey, each of which was to have a civilian Governor; and over two military territories: Niger and Mauritania.[5]

Meanwhile, France's colonial boundaries in West Africa had been fixed by a series of agreements with Germany in 1885, Portugal in 1886 and Britain in 1889, but it was not

[3] Cf. the *Bulletin du Comité de l'Afrique Française* for January 1891.
[4] Cf. Henri Brunschwig, *Mythes et réalités de l'impérialisme colonial français* (Paris, Armand Colin, 1960), pp. 116–137.
[5] Cf. Général Duboc, *L'epopée coloniale en Afrique occidentale française* (Paris, Editions Edgar Malfère, 1938), pp. 348–354.

until 1900 that the frontier between Mauritania and Rio de Oro was definitely fixed with Spain. The tribes of Mauritania itself submitted after several campaigns to Coppolani, who became the first 'Commissaire du Gouvernement' when the area was declared a 'territoire civil' in 1904. But his assassination in 1905 led to further trouble and Mauritania was not pacified until some ten years later.

II THE COLONIAL SITUATION

IT has been said that the welter of peoples living in French West Africa is such as to defy accurate classification.[1] In addition to the thirteen main African tribes, the territories formerly in the A.O.F. contain three main 'white' or mulatto groups—of Berber or Arab origin but with a variable admixture of Negro blood—who constitute the essentially nomadic elements in the region's population.

The political history of contemporary West Africa is complicated by the fact that its peoples live in east-west groupings, whereas the political pattern imposed by the colonising powers is north-south. If frontiers are the scars of history, the key to the understanding of African boundaries is the speed with which they were defined. Most were decided between 1884 and 1919, and great lengths were agreed upon in each treaty.[2] Very seldom were these international boundaries established with any respect for the unity of African peoples: one-third, if measured according to length, are geometrical. They were imposed upon indigenous societies whose feelings have always been sensitive about matters of land delimitation and ownership. The result is that tribes historically antagonistic to one another have been linked, whilst homogeneous linguistic and racial groups have been rent apart. The 'scramble for Africa' took place at a time when knowledge of the ethnography, terrain and natural economy of the continent's interior was extremely limited. The unity of African peoples was not respected and the following tragic anomalies were among the many which followed: the Hausa people were divided by the Niger-Nigeria boundary

[1] V. Thompson and R. Adloff, *French West Africa* (London, George Allen and Unwin, 1958), p. 22.
[2] R. J. Harrison Church, in *The Changing World. Studies in Political Geography*, edited by W. Gordon East and A. E. Moodie (London, George G. Harrap, 1956), p. 744.

whilst the Kru people were divided by the Ivory Coast-Liberia boundary; even more drastic was the partition in 1919 of the Ewe people between Togo under French Mandate and Togoland under British Mandate. These Mandates were transformed into Trusteeships from 1946 until 1960 and 1957 respectively. The Niger-Nigerian boundary cuts across natural trade routes which had been used for centuries and the Dahomey-Nigeria boundary crosses the lagoon waterway between Porto-Novo and Lagos. But 'the ethnic march-lands cut by boundaries are broad; and historically they are significant as the great ritual and political centres of Africa—if only to illustrate the confusion in perspective between ethnography and post-colonial nationalism'.[3]

By 1900 the era of conquest had virtually ended in West Africa and the French were confronted with the difficult task of consolidating their gains, by means of political and economic organisation. The first attempt at union under a Governor-General, in 1895, was both limited and prudent for, despite the creation of a 'Conseil Supérieur', each colony retained its full autonomy. Four years later a closer union was imposed by decree when it became apparent that a federal budget would be required to provide for the construction of a railway from each of the coastal outlets to the common centre, the Niger Basin. Without effective land communications, commerce could never develop. In 1899 the sprawling land mass of the Soudan was divided amongst Senegal, Upper-Senegal-Niger, Guinea, Ivory Coast and Dahomey. As a result, each of the coastal colonies was given access to an interior market.

The Governor-General who administered Senegal directly, from Dakar instead of from Saint-Louis as heretofore, continued not to have any effective independent power in the other four colonies which, though nominally under a civilian governor, were in fact controlled by the Colonial

[3] C. W. Newbury, *The Western Slave Coast and its Rulers* (Oxford, Clarendon Press, 1961), preface, p. viii.

Minister in Paris. But as a result of the reforms of 1902–1904 introduced on Gaston Doumergue's initiative, and followed by the appointment of the able and energetic Ernest Roume as Governor-General, an effective 'Gouvernement-Général' was established at Dakar, with its own budget and its corps of officials.[4]

The new federal Government, relieved of direct responsibility for Senegal, very soon undermined the various local governors' authority by frequent interference. A similar centralising trend would have manifested itself in the individual colonies had it not been for the usual inaccessibility and autarchy of such officials as the 'commandants de cercle'. Their remoteness in distant outposts preserved them from constant intervention and hence enabled them to make independent and swift decisions concerning the wide variety of problems they were expected to tackle.

Throughout the new A.O.F. federation, emphasis came increasingly to be placed on the Federal Government, particularly with regard to policy-making. Not only did Doumergue's reforms forge an administrative unit, but they also made possible the economic development of the Federation. They thus constitute the most important landmark in its history.

As a result, a federal budget and five local ones were linked to the Governor-General and to his Lieutenant-Governors. Each colony was granted financial and administrative autonomy, though certain powers were specifically reserved to the Governor-General. In 1903, for instance, a loan of 65 million francs was raised for the economic development of the Federation. The appropriation of this sum by the federal authorities in Dakar, as well as that of the revenue derived from the new tariff imposed in 1908 to finance construction of public works, constituted a more effective and direct exercise of power than any of the

---

[4] Doumergue was Colonial Minister in the Combes Government (1902–1905).

co-ordinating functions considered to be the Governor-General's essential prerogative.

The construction of a network of rail and road communications proved an obvious prerequisite for the establishment of what Pierre Lyautey has described as 'une fusion d'intérêts, une communauté de rapports', throughout the new Federation. This made for centralisation. But Senegal's special privileges made it imperative that the component territories be allowed a degree of autonomy, for France's oldest African outpost would never have tolerated the more recently acquired colonies being considered of equal status. By the turn of the century, Senegal had reached a very much more advanced stage of political development, with elective institutions and a relatively complex administrative system, than any other area of tropical Africa governed by a European power. France's 'Code civil' had been promulgated in Senegal as far back as 1833. According to the declaration then made, every person born free and resident in the colony was to enjoy the rights granted by the 'Code civil' to French citizens.[5] The creation of the four 'communes de plein exercice' (that is to say territories under direct administration) had its origin in this decision taken by Louis-Philippe's Government. The four communes were Saint-Louis, Gorée, Rufisque and Dakar,[6] whose 'originaires', of both European and African stock, were endowed since 1848 with the same adult male suffrage as was introduced in France. The French constitution of 1848 provided for the election of twelve colonial deputies (of whom one from Senegal) and although this provision was abrogated during the Second Empire, it was reintroduced in 1871.

African inhabitants of the 'communes' were likewise entitled to the retention of their own (usually Muslim) law,

[5] Cf. Pierre Lyautey, *L'Empire colonial français* (Paris, Les Editions de France, 1931), p. 170.
[6] Dakar was founded as late as 1857 by Faidherbe. The 'communes' of Gorée and Dakar were amalgamated in 1946.

in place of the French 'Code civil', in such matters as marriage and inheritance. This special status, enjoyed by virtue of the inhabitants' birth in the territory, was granted in 1848, when a Muslim tribunal was set up in Saint-Louis.

Although these 'communes' covered only a small area, they are of great significance in the history of French colonial rule in West Africa and are in a considerable measure responsible for the definite affinity existing between Senegal and France. Yet efforts were made from time to time by the French administration to deprive the 'originaires' of their special privileges, on the ground that they were not French citizens. In 1890 the territory 'de plein exercice' was restrictively defined and the remainder of the colony of Senegal proclaimed a 'protectorate', whose inhabitants were French subjects (as were those of the other territories of French tropical Africa), not French citizens.[7] In view of the intermittent attempts to deprive the 'originaires' of their rights, perhaps the greatest of Blaise Diagne's[8] achievements was the passage of the law of 1916 confirming that 'the natives of the four communes of Senegal and their descendants are and remain French citizens', whilst defining the liability of the 'citoyens indigènes français' to conscription throughout the colony.

Other institutional and administrative features peculiar to it further emphasised Senegal's favoured position. Between 1872 and 1887 the four 'communes' were endowed with the institutions of local self-government, thus reproducing the pattern of French municipalities. Later, the urban organisation of Dakar developed independently: the government services came to be controlled by an official Administrator, whereas the Port, under a special Commissioner, had its own budget.[9]

[7] Cf. W. J. M. Mackenzie and Kenneth Robinson, Editors, *Five Elections in Africa* (Oxford, Clarendon Press, 1960), p. 290.
[8] The first African to represent Senegal in Paris (1914–1934) and Under-Secretary for the Colonies during the First World War.
[9] Cf. Lord Hailey, *An African Survey* (London, Oxford University Press, 1957), p. 544.

As from 1879, Senegal had an elected 'Conseil Général', with twenty members, which imposed taxation and approved the budget of the territory under direct administration. In 1920, when the two administrative divisions of Senegal were combined, the 'Conseil Général' was replaced by a 'Conseil Colonial' whose powers extended to the entire colony. These powers related principally to control of the territorial budget, but were in fact restricted by the distinction between obligatory and optional expenditure, for the former of which they had to make provision. But the 'Conseil Colonial' had no legislative powers. Twenty of its members were elected by the electorate of the former 'Conseil Général', that is to say by the 'citoyens français' under adult male suffrage, whilst the other half consisted of native chiefs chosen by the canton and provincial chiefs of the former 'protectorate'. As paid agents of the Government the chiefs tended to form an official opposition to the 'originaires'. So much so that in 1925 the membership was modified to include twenty-four members elected by the 'originaires', with only sixteen chiefs. An additional change of emphasis was given to the 'Conseil's' composition in 1939, when a new group of eighteen members who were noncitizens was elected by all French subjects in Senegal who had completed their military service. But the 'Conseil Colonial', together with the elected municipal councils of the four 'communes', was suppressed by the Vichy Government in 1940.[10]

The Federation itself was enlarged after the First World War to include Upper Volta in 1919, Mauritania in 1920 and Niger in 1922. In 1921 the mandated territory of Togo (formerly a German possession) was granted autonomy by France and its administration, under a 'Commissaire de la République', remained entirely separate from that of Dahomey or Upper Volta.

[10] Cf. R. L. Buell, *The Native Problem in Africa* (New York, The Macmillan Co., 1928) vol. I, pp. 946–982 and Mackenzie and Robinson, pp. 290–291.

A 'Conseil de Gouvernement' advised the A.O.F.'s Governor-General. It was composed of the Governors of the component colonies, the Commissioner for Togo, and seven other official members, together with the Deputy for Senegal, the four members of the 'Conseil Supérieur de la France d'Outre-Mer' in Paris elected by the A.O.F.'s 'citoyens', four non-citizens from A.O.F. and four members elected by the Chambers of Commerce and Dakar's 'Conseil Municipal'. This advisory body met annually and considered both the federal budget and that of each colony. Within each colony, except Senegal, a 'Conseil d'Administration' advised the Governor, who consulted it on local administrative and budgetary problems. In Guinea, Soudan, the Ivory Coast and Dahomey, these 'Conseils' comprised three official members, two French citizens elected by the Chambers of Agriculture and Commerce respectively, and three non-citizens elected by non-citizens with special qualifications and who included a number of senior chiefs. In Niger and Mauritania, on the other hand, the 'Conseils' which were set up comprised only unofficial members nominated by the Governors, in addition to the official members.

The objective of French colonial policy has always differed in one fundamental respect from that of the British. Whereas the latter eschewed any definition of the content of self-government, which Britain's colonial dependencies were being trained to achieve, since any rigid definition could never cover all the possibilities involved where so many units at varying stages of political progress were concerned, French Governments, from the days of Richelieu and Colbert onwards, invariably posited as axiomatic the basic concept of the unity between metropolitan France and her dependencies. This policy led to the granting of French citizenship to certain non-European inhabitants of colonial territories, together with direct representation in parliamentary institutions in Paris. Conversely this conception, which reached its apogee in the

Constitution of the 'Union Française' in 1946, implied the maintenance of considerable legislative and executive control from France. This control was in practice somewhat mitigated by the gradual extension of local government authority in the dependencies. Thus France's African subjects—namely all Africans apart from the 'citoyens' who numbered only some 80,000 in 1936—enjoyed no rights of representation, but lived under an authoritarian system in which public law was the product not of legislation, but, under the terms of the 'senatus-consulte' of 1854, of executive decree.

Although the Act of Napoleon III's Senate was, at the time when it was passed, constructive and claimed to be 'propre à réaliser les intentions d'un gouvernement libéral et sensé, basé sur l'étude des faits et conforme à l'état des esprits, ouvrant aux hommes intelligents et devoués l'accès des affairs du pays, conciliant dans une juste mesure les intérêts de l'autorité et ceux de la liberté', by the time Pétain headed the Vichy Government, it appeared merely jejune.

The main body of the 'senatus-consulte' of 3 May 1854, related to Martinique, Guadeloupe and Reunion as the last to survive from amongst France's earliest colonial possessions, but Article 18 applied to the other dependencies. This stated that 'elles seront régies par décret de l'empereur jusqu'à ce qu'il ait été statué à leur égard par un senatus-consulte'; but the latter never took shape. As a result, these colonies remained subject to a completely authoritarian regime. No role was assigned to the legislature or to the 'Conseil d'Etat' in Paris, as far as these dependencies were concerned, though the Governor-General himself was empowered to issue orders ('arrêtés').[11]

This 'senatus-consulte' was thus a reflection of the centralising tendencies of the French polity which, as de Tocqueville and Pagès stressed, were already manifest

[11] Cf. Arthur Girault, *Principes de colonisation et de législation coloniale* (Paris, Recueil Sirey, 1929) 5th edition, vol. 2, Second Part, Chapter IV.

under the 'ancien régime'. They were given greater cohesion and developed consistently under the First Empire, many of whose 'légistes' had served in the 'Parlements' under Louis XVI. Lord Hailey relates how 'the most distinguished teacher in the "Ecole Coloniale" from 1889 to 1932, M. Paul Dislère, used to insist that the primary object to be attained in the Colonies was the creation of real French Administrative Departments'. It was this type of approach that Lyautey violently excoriated when, in a letter to Chailley-Bert dated 1901, he described the 'maladie de l'Uniformité' as 'le plus grave péril'.[12]

The French never discriminated against Africans on racial grounds and French territories never witnessed such phenomena as separate toilet facilities for Europeans, Asians and Africans as in Kenya and Natal, or such practices as the enforcement of curfews and the obligation on Africans to hold passes as in Kenya, Rhodesia, South Africa and Elisabethville in the Belgian Congo. But until 1946, all Africans except the privileged 'citoyens' were classed as French subjects. As such, they enjoyed no right of representation, no access to the higher ranks of the administration or to universities and were offered few opportunities to qualify for secondary education. Until 1946, again, Africans could be drafted into brigades for compulsory labour, usually for public works. Reliance was placed mainly on the system of 'prestation', a tax payable in the form of a definite amount of labour; in addition, use was sometimes made of military conscripted labour, whilst in theory, after 1848, vagabonds were declared at the disposal of the State for employment. In practice, however, little recourse was had to the provisions of the vagrancy law.[13] One of the most hated features of the colonial system in French West Africa was the 'indigénat', the special legal provision whereby Africans could be tried and sentenced on

[12] Maréchal Lyautey, *Lettres du Sud de Madagascar* (Paris, Armand Colin, 1935), p. 211.
[13] Cf. Lord Hailey, pp. 1362–1370.

the spot by French administrators. As Mr. Fenner Brockway has said, 'nothing so pierces the personality as the humiliation of being treated as a lesser human being'.[14]

Yet West Africans formerly under French rule have expressed, on balance, very little rancour against France; nor have they so far manifested any strong racial feelings against Europeans personally such as have been reported from the Congo and Angola, from Kenya, Nyasaland and Northern Rhodesia. Some of their leaders have fought the French politically and have resented the latter's authoritarian rule, but they have not attacked Frenchmen as individuals. Thus, in an Africa now bedevilled by extreme forms of nationalism, de Gaulle's concept of a 'French Community', however much eroded, still survives, for at all times the French have thought of Africans, basically, as human beings and potential equals. But it was among the French-speaking intellectuals that the concept of *négritude* first came to the fore as early as the years 1932–1935.

Since there were not always enough French officials available, power was frequently devolved to African chiefs and traditional native authorities. This did not mean that the system evolved out of Sir Frederick (later Lord) Lugard's experiment in Northern Nigeria, between 1900 and 1906 of 'indirect rule' based on the use of the traditional native authorities, was ever reproduced by the French. The French made their presence felt through the provincial 'cercles', of which there were 105 in 1950, with 173 'subdivisions'.[15]

In the rural areas only the chiefs were educated. Preferment was often given to the sons of traditional chiefs, for whom the 'Ecole des Fils des Chefs' was founded at Saint-Louis. But since the aim of French administrators was to replace descent by merit, as the main criterion for recruitment and service, this institution was superseded by the

[14] *Observer* 'Profile' of 28 January 1962.
[15] Cf. *L'Afrique occidentale française* (Paris, Les Carnets d'Outre-Mer, 1951) p. 40.

Ecole Normale William-Ponty in Dakar. The chiefs became
in effect French officials who were paid salaries or
given a share of the money they collected, whilst acting as
mouth-pieces of the administration. When a powerful chief
died, he was frequently replaced by a French official or by a
semi-literate canton or village chief, a willing tool of the
French. A 'commandement indigène', as it came to be
called, was thus organised to mediate between rural Africans
and the French administrators.

Traditional chiefs tended to survive in the savannah
regions on account of the more integrated political systems
which obtained there in pre-colonial times. At the beginning
of the twentieth century, labour for the Thiès-Niger and
the Cotonou and Dahomey railways was procured by orders
directed to the chiefs, who contracted for it from the
villages. But it was French practice to dismiss an official
chief, however traditionally based his power may have
been, who did not meet the administration's approval.
Empirical methods were replaced by what van Vollenhoven
called 'la colonisation routinière'.

The first of the many 'Circulaires' of cardinal importance
for French policy was issued from Dakar in 1909 by the
Governor-General, William Ponty. It formulated 'une
politique des races' based on the destruction of the great
paramountcies in order to establish closer contacts between
the French administration and the African population.
The policy was further developed in 1911 and 1913. This
was not altogether surprising for as a former Governor,
Hubert Deschamps, has stressed 'le Français pratique mal
l'administration indirecte. L'inéfficacité, la concussion,
l'injustice le révoltent et l'impatientent; du contrôle il
passe constamment à l'intervention.'[16] But the shortage
of trained personnel, a major stumbling-block to any
effective implementation of Ponty's plans, was aggravated

[16] *Les méthodes et les doctrines coloniales de la France* (Paris, Armand Colin,
1953) p. 211.

by the First World War, during which the A.O.F. provided France with 175,000 'tirailleurs'.[17]

Until about 1925, French West Africa produced chiefly forest products such as gum, rubber and ivory. After that date, gum remained the principal product of Mauritania, but the A.O.F.'s rubber, obtained from wild trees and creepers, could no longer compete with Asiatic cultivated rubber. On the other hand, the marketing of ordinary timber and precious woods was considerably developed in the Ivory Coast, which contains some 120,000 square kilometres of virgin forest. As the European inhabitants were few in number—about 32,000—the progress of cultivation depended mainly on Africans. The administration encouraged Africans to grow varied and better crops, at least for export. The richest areas were those producing cash crops for the European, mainly French, market.

Vegetable oils are amongst the most important of the region's products. The ground nut is the principal source of the prosperity of Senegal, where it has been cultivated since about 1890; the Ivory Coast and Dahomey produce mainly palm oil and palm kernels, together with coffee and cocoa. Guinea is rich in bananas and pineapples. The European inhabitants were particularly eager to cultivate cotton, since most areas, with the exception of the excessively dry districts bordering the Sahara and the excessively wet districts along the coast, were suitable for this crop. Ginning stations were established, the transport of cotton after ginning was organised, the quality of native cotton was improved, and American cotton was introduced and water supplied through irrigation.

The local industries producing leather and cotton goods were useful but of little economic significance. They were— and are still—more highly developed among the Mandé of the interior than among the populations of the coast, since the latter were always able to obtain clothing and

[17] Cf. C. W. Newbury, pp. 203–204.

other articles from the European trading stores. In addition, there was a considerable amount of internal trading, the principal commodities sold being salt, cola nuts and European goods.

The French favoured individual as opposed to tribal tenure of land and planned to base West Africa on peasant production. Thus in the territories of the A.O.F., Africans had a clear title of ownership to their land.

Two broad, but incompatible, principles have characterised the different views, held at different times, by Frenchmen on the crucial issue of the ideal relationship between Europeans and Africans: 'assimilation' on the one hand and 'association' on the other. Until the closing decades of the nineteenth century, French policy was based on the concept of 'assimilation' which regarded colonies as integral, though non-contiguous, parts of France. This was first given effect by the 'Convention' in the Constitution of the Year III.[18] In this, Frenchmen in 1795 were merely putting into practice philosophical theories which had been accepted as fundamental premises of political thought by the 'philosophes': belief in the power of reason and in the concept of universal man. But the humanitarianism and idealism underlying the principle of assimilation could not thrive unaided in the imperialist *ambiance* which developed in the following century. This does not mean that assimilation was 'nothing' but a rationalisation of direct exploitation. But it is certainly true that the idea of religious conversion, evident during the seventeenth century,[19] was first transmuted into political and cultural assimilation and then into the more detailed concept of association.

Cultural imperialism is part of the French tradition, a heritage from France's cultural paramountcy in the

[18] Cf. *Constitution du 5 Fructidor*, An III; Titre Premier, Division du Territoire.
[19] The royal edicts of 1635 and 1642 stated that the natives, once converted to Catholicism, were to be considered citizens and natural Frenchmen.

eighteenth century. The policy of assimilation is one of its aspects, for its advocates aspired to shape colonial society and institutions in the mother country's image. As Rupert Emerson has put it, it fitted 'the French genius in the past to assume that the people of their colonies could become Frenchmen and to aim at their integration into the homogeneous society of a single Greater France revolving about Paris.'[20] One of the advantages of this, in theory at least, was to have been the provision of a uniform colonial administration.

By the end of the nineteenth century, however, assimilation came to be analysed dispassionately by leading authorities on colonial problems, some of whom unceremoniously rejected it. It was no longer considered relevant to France's new and highly diversified colonial empire (which by then comprised three different categories of status: colony, federation and protectorate) and was condemned as rigid and unscientific. Instead, a more flexible and realistic colonial policy was urged upon French Governments by a new generation of colonial thinkers who had observed the anchylosis in the Philippines produced by the Spanish colonial system. Some of these writers, such as Joseph Chailley-Bert (the great Paul Bert's son-in-law) and Jules Harmand, derived inspiration from a critical study of the British and Dutch colonial systems, in both of which a more empirical approach to problems and peoples was discernible.[21]

The theory of evolution by natural selection provided grounds for ruthlessness in the thought of the naturally successful people of Europe about those they regarded as more primitive. It was, they felt, part of nature's plan that the more capable only should survive. With this ruthlessness

[20] Rupert Emerson, *From Empire to Nation* (Cambridge, Harvard University Press, 1960) p. 69.
[21] For a valuable and well-documented study of French thought on colonial theory at the end of the nineteenth century and after, see Raymond F. Betts, *Assimilation and Association in French Colonial Theory* (New York, Columbia University Press, 1961).

went a development which at first sight seemed to contradict it, a growing realisation among anthropologists that the culture of a people forms a whole from which single items cannot be abstracted or changed without damage to the whole. But this was harnessed to the ruthlessness inspired by Darwinism; if the culture was a whole, you could not really apply the old concept of the possibility of assimilation and the potential equality of men. The individual must sink or survive with his culture, and if that was demonstrably more primitive, then so was he. Thus the change from the official policy of assimilation to a new policy of association, though it led sometimes to slight liberalisation of governmental forms, carried with it often a new contempt for the individual.

Arguing in favour of a more flexible native policy, the new generation of colonial thinkers wished to enlist co-operation through respect for local institutions and customs. 'Association' was the word most often used to describe the method advocated and it was conceived as the antidote to 'assimilation', which was deemed to have failed. Close co-operation was to be achieved by encouraging rather than submerging the particular ethnic, political and economic characteristics of any given area. Practical considerations also contributed to the acceptance of the new theory. Since France's empire was spread round the globe, the co-operation and intelligent use of local labour became essential to the development of each dependency's economic resources. The notion of French civilisation, implicit in assimilation, had failed to transform the average native who was more often exploited or ignored than he was educated. Realising this, French colonial theorists sought to make France's overseas empire a viable entity.

The discussion on the relative merits of assimilation and association which went on from 1890—when assimilation was last given wide sanction at the 'Congrès National Colonial'—onwards, proved more than academic. More autonomy in regional affairs became evident and the acceptance of a less rigid policy by officials in Paris ensued. Furthermore, a more conscious interest in the overseas colonies and in their multitudinous problems was aroused.

Not the least important result was the gradual emergence of a concept of the role to be played by the new élite in this system of indirect rule, which association came to imply. The importance of the élite, as the go-between for the French and African populations is evident, for any policy of association would create attendant problems such as that of the 'déracinés'. Félix Eboué, for one, in French Equatorial Africa, immediately sensed the dangers of what Maurice Barrès stigmatised as 'la liberté désolée de l'âne sauvage'.

Theories and practices formulated in France were not invariably or uncritically applied in overseas possessions. Every period of French colonial history reveals such discrepancies, for administrators on the spot proved as empirical on occasion as their counterparts from other countries. Like Gustave Le Bon, French colonial administrators realised that a people cannot be transformed 'à coup de décrets'—though France has not pursued the same tradition of elasticity in constitutional matters as Britain.

Lyautey wrote that 'si cinq années d'expériences coloniales nous ont appris quelque chose, c'est à coup sûr le plus complet éclécticisme quant à l'étiquette du régime', for in the colonies 'l'imprévu est la règle et la décision est la nécessité quotidienne'.[22] Nevertheless, the debate between the exponents of assimilation and the champions of association caused the French to become more intensely aware of the problems of modern imperialism. In the words of an American historian, 'the importance of a method, a "science" of colonialism, as it were, designed to fuse the interests of the two peoples placed in contact by the act of imperialism itself, was henceforth recognised'.[23] But although association became the official colonial policy after

[22] Lyautey, *Lettres du Tonkin et de Madagascar 1894–1899* (Paris, Armand Colin, 1946) pp. 629–630.
[23] Betts, p. 175.

1918, 'the ghost of assimilation lingered on and could still be seen flitting in and out of French colonial affairs'.[24] This is obvious; Paul Mus, writing as late as 1954, referred to assimilation in the following terms: 'elle n'atteint pas l'Afrique, qui se replie sur elle-même et instruit à nouveau ses affaires par coutume, chaque fois qu'elle le peut. Les anciens et les chefs arbitrent, les ordalies traditionnelles reprennent de l'actualité: par l'eau, le feu ou le poison.'[25]

Both principles were opposed to the aim of colonial self-government as pursued by Britain,[26] but the concept of assimilation was more in keeping with the strong unitary and *etatiste* tendencies of French constitutional practice. Moreover, the system of having inspectors sent out periodically from Paris to the colonies made centralisation a reality. 'At every stage, the development of the French Empire reflects less the Republican and democratic nature of modern France than the nationalist, authoritarian character of the social classes which have been most concerned with its creation.'[27]

By 1939 the official system had become fossilised and presented many points of danger. For though assimilation was virtually repudiated, the concept of association which had been extolled with enthusiasm was fast becoming a mere label, barely concealing an atmosphere of stubborn conservatism. 'Un large souffle nouveau était nécessaire. Il vint d'un choc terrible, la guerre de 1940, qui chassa la France outre-mer'.[28]

---

[24] *Ibid.*, p. 165.

[25] *Le destin de l'union française* (Paris, Editions du Seuil) p. 286.

[26] But Albert Sarraut, a former Governor-General of Indo-China and a statesman of considerable distinction who, as a Radical, served in several ministries, had viewed as early as 1923 the prospects of self-government with complete equanimity. Cf. his *La mise en valeur des colonies françaises*, which is a very remarkable work.

[27] David Thomson, *Democracy in France* (London, Oxford University Press, 1946) p. 167.

[28] H. Deschamps, p. 176.

III THE REJECTION OF COLONIALISM

THE rise of nationalism amongst non-European peoples is a consequence of the spread of Western European civilisation, which brought with it ideas of destruction of foreign rule. By 1939 the peoples of the states formerly under European domination had come to desire possession of the secrets and sources of the white man's supremacy. The newly-rising leadership of 'évolués' sought to come to terms with Western civilisation by achieving mastery of the mainsprings of power. Amongst the most politically conscious, some believed that the introduction of Western parliamentary democracy symbolised the attainment of political maturity; others looked to Moscow for guidance and inspiration; a minority, from whose ranks Gandhi stood out most vividly, refused to regard the West as a model of any relevance and denied its intrinsic superiority.

The Second World War let loose 'self-determination' as a vital desideratum for the non-European peoples under alien rule.[1] It crystallised the nationalist claims which had been diversely expressed during the inter-war years and thus ensured that their assertion would evoke the requisite response under the watchful eye of the United Nations. The United Nations Charter explicitly endorsed colonial emancipation as a primary objective. Provision was made for the creation of a Trusteeship Council, half of whose total membership was to be constituted by powers which did not themselves own colonies. The Articles of the Charter relating to colonial matters represented a degree of

[1] The principle of self-determination had first been propounded, of course, by Allied leaders—and more especially by Wilson—during the First World War but it had been regarded, as a result of tacit agreement, as a matter of application only in Europe. But its inherently revolutionary implications were not slow to spread amongst subject peoples the world over.

compromise, due to the conflicting viewpoints amongst the Allies, but they undoubtedly implied the recognition that the colonial problem should be resolved by international agreement. The most significant innovation was the 'Declaration Regarding Non-Self-Governing Territories' which entitled the General Assembly of the United Nations to debate the colonial powers' achievements or malpractices.[2]

Within the United Nations itself, there emerged an Afro-Asian bloc which soon began to act as the self-appointed and vigilant champion of non-Europeans in general and of peoples still subject to colonialism in particular. Whereas in the twenties even revelations of serious abuses in colonial territories were seldom considered sufficient to justify condemnation, within the space of one generation the system itself had come to be stigmatised as wholly intolerable.

A ground-swell of anti-colonialism swept throughout the underdeveloped world and as a result the balance of world forces has undergone a fundamental transformation. The memorable failure of the Anglo-French attack on Egypt in 1956 merely underlined the drastic change in the power-structure which had recently occurred beyond the confines of Europe.

French colonialism reached its nadir under the Vichy régime. Forced labour throughout French tropical Africa was intensified. Colonies were made to send a very much higher proportion of their production to German-occupied France. The outstanding loyalty of Africans to the Free French movement and their refusal to make political capital out of France's crippled condition, were the background to the Brazzaville conference of 30 January to 8 February 1944. The capital of French Equatorial Africa was chosen as its site because of that Federation's complete freedom from any form of association with Pétain, to whose Government the A.O.F. under Pierre Boisson had, in contrast,

[2] Cf. Chapter XI, Article 73, sub-clauses (d) and (e).

remained loyal until the Allied landings in North Africa in 1942.

The political history of French-speaking West Africa may be said to date from the Brazzaville conference. As 'Commissaire aux Colonies', in the 'Comité français de libération nationale' set up by General de Gaulle, René Pleven stated at the conference:

Dans la grande France, il n'y a ni peuple à affranchir, ni discrimination raciale à abolir ... Il y a des populations que nous entendons conduire, d'étapes en étapes, à une personnalité plus complète, à l'affranchissement politique, mais qui n'entendent connaître d'autre indépendance que l'indépendance de la France.

The Governor-General of the A.E.F., Félix Eboué, of African descent though born not in Africa but in French Guiana, and a former Governor of Tchad, was the leading figure at the conference which brought together eighteen Governors but not one African leader. It was Eboué who, shortly before, had paid special attention to the incipient African bourgeoisie, and who had suggested a 'Statut des Notables Evolués' who 'deviendraient ainsi de véritables citoyens de la colonie et, comme tels, appelés à faire, sous notre contrôle, leurs preuves dans l'administration de leur propre commune'.[3] Such views were very much more advanced than those previously expressed by the *pétainiste* Boisson in his 'Trois Directives de Colonisation Africaine' issued in August 1941: 'Coloniser, c'est essentiellement faire avancer les sociétés indigènes dans les voies que nous avons choisies pour elles ... Ce sont à la fois les élites et les masses qui doivent nous suivre'.

The African élite eagerly awaited the outcome of the conference. Never had its hopes stood so high since the day when it learnt the news of the formation of Léon Blum's Popular Front Government in 1936. The accession to power, in Paris, of members of the Socialist Party and of the 'Ligue des Droits de l'Homme', known to favour radical

[3] *La Nouvelle Politique Indigène*, Circulaire, November 1941.

reforms throughout the colonies, had galvanised the
African intelligentsia. The appointment of Marius Moutet
as Colonial Minister,[4] who created a 'Commission
d'Enquête' and, together with Robert Delavignette, drew up
a programme of local works that would benefit Africans,
seemed to herald a new age for the peoples subject to
French rule. But Blum's Government, impaled on the
'five eights' (the forty-hour week) by right-wing senators
and deputies, was short-lived.

One of the most significant results of Blum's resignation
in 1937 was a widening of the rift between the local élites and
the policy-makers in Paris. Intellectuals formed in the
French educational system demanded independence for
Tunisia and Viet-Nam; in Algeria and Madagascar, they
claimed the right to the status and benefits of French
citizenship. In the A.O.F., where an organised political
party did not emerge until 1947, members of the African
élite, many of whom had made their way from their village
school to regional primary school or upper primary school,[5]
established permanent contact with one another through
town associations. Student clubs and alumni groups were
formed and enabled their members to discuss the political
issues which they could not raise constitutionally. The
'Voix du Montagnard', formed by Fulani students at
William-Ponty, developed into the Guinea political club
'Amicale Gilbert Vieillard' and later into the Guinea
Socialist Party. Similarly, graduates of the Catholic
seminary at Ouagadougou organised the 'Union Voltaïque',
the party which insisted on the separation of Upper Volta

---

[4] Later Minister of Overseas Territories in the Gouin, Bidault, Blum and
Ramadier Governments (January 1946-October 1947) and Senator for
Soudan in 1947.

[5] Only a small proportion of students—such as Ouëzzin Coulibaly
(political director of the R.D.A.); Modibo Keita (President of Mali);
Diallo Sayfoulaye (President of the Guinea National Assembly);
Mathieu Ekra (Minister of Information of the Ivory Coast) and Assogba
Oké (Foreign Minister of Dahomey)—succeeded in entering the principal
federal secondary school, the Ecole Normale William-Ponty.

from the Ivory Coast in 1947.[6] But in the Ivory Coast it would seem that regional associations with political interests were not formed until after 1945.[7] Elsewhere, it was through such associations that the élite acquired the experience which served them in good stead when post-war opportunities enabled many of them to emerge as political leaders within the existing territorial groupings.

Political consciousness thus gradually developed on a fairly large scale during the inter-war period. And if it is true to say that, as a whole, French West Africans approved of the policy of assimilation since it postulated the essential equality of Africans with Frenchmen and thus implied the removal of the hindrances that maintained inequality, it is also true that there were some keener minds amongst the 'évolués' who, like Léopold Sédar Senghor, wished to assimilate without being assimilated. Such men realised that assimilation implied the continuing subordination of African interests to French policies. The élite, made up of the intelligentsia and professional men, rendered articulate the inchoate feelings of the masses: disaffection and grievances produced by the pressures and tensions arising out of the desire for development set in motion by the colonial power. The intellectual élite was often joined by the rising indigenous entrepreneurs, many of whom had become prosperous; but they seldom took a share in the leadership of the nationalist movements with which they sympathised. In addition, it was joined increasingly by workers' leaders, though it was not until 1937 that they were able to form trade unions.

Yet the economic aspects of colonialism were not as significant as the political and social in determining the nationalist fervour in French Africa. And this is so despite the fact that changes introduced by Europeans in the economic structure of the territories—the most fundamental

[6] Cf. Hodgkin and Schachter, p. 386.
[7] Cf. F. J. Amon d'Aby, *La Côte d'Ivoire dans la cité africaine* (Paris, Editions Larose, 1951) p. 36.

of which was their transformation to a money economy—contributed largely to the disruption of the older societies.

Nationalism has always been a largely urban phenomenon, and Africa has proved no exception; it is in its towns, whose growth has been one of the outstanding social developments of recent decades, that regular contact with Europeans has brought to the local community a fuller realisation of its contrasting standards of living. Professor Balandier has emphasised the special orientation in race relations in Africa produced by urban contact. The political maturity of the African town-dweller was developed through his daily experience of the dominant role of the Europeans and of the striking disproportion between the modes and level of life of the two communities.[8]   A pre-capitalist community has little to contribute to capitalist enterprise in towns except the provision of a steady supply of unskilled labour. The peasantry in the countryside have seldom been as conscious of the higher standard of living enjoyed by the white community, except when called upon to do military service abroad.

The French-speaking West African knowledge of political thought and its experience of political organisation were derived from contact with liberal-minded Catholic missionaries or with members of the French Socialist and Communist Parties, many of whom were teachers in the A.O.F.   In 1943, an organisation called the 'Groupes d'Etudes Communistes' was set up in Dakar, Conakry, Abidjan, Bamako and Bobo-Dioulasso.   Though only a few Africans became doctrinaire Marxists, the political leaders now in control of the Governments of Guinea, Mali and the Ivory Coast adapted Marxist methodology and techniques to their local requirements.

The 'Groupes' also encouraged the determination of the younger members of the élite to develop an essentially African philosophy and cultural mores of their own. This was a natural reaction on the part of intelligent young men

[8] Cf. *Sociologie des Brazzavilles noires* (Paris, Armand Colin, 1955).

brought up in a society in which education was controlled largely by a foreign State whose primary object was the dissemination of French culture. With the exception of the mandated territories of Togo and the French Cameroons, in which teachers in mission schools were permitted to use the vernacular, the French language was made the medium of all instruction.[9] Education was completely inter-racial.[10] In addition, military training was compulsory: Africans, consequently, were expected by French administrative practice to show loyalty to cultural and patriotic values alien to their own distinctive, traditional heritage.

Such factors help to account for the remarkable intellectual enthusiasm and vigour engendered by the rapid acceptance of the philosophy of *négritude*. Anyone who studies the works of the post-war writers who developed under the ægis of the journal and publishing-house, *Présence Africaine* (established in Paris and directed by Alioune Diop, 'chef de cabinet' of Senegal's Minister of Youth and Sports), must be struck by the quality of the thought and writing, even if he is critical of the partisanship sometimes displayed. This new cultural flowering was preceded by a more modest group of revivalists, which included in its number the novelist Bernard Dadié and the playwright Cofi Gadeau, both from the Ivory Coast, and Keïta Fodeba, the producer of African ballets, from Guinea. The greatest of all the 'évolués', however, was the President of Senegal, Léopold Sédar Senghor, who was born in 1906 at Joal, the son of a prosperous Serer family. Senghor was educated at the Catholic Mission and at the *lycée* in Dakar, and later at the *lycée* Louis-le-Grand in Paris, at the Faculté des Lettres, at the Institut d'Ethnologie and at the Ecole Pratique des Hautes Etudes, at the Sorbonne. He was the first African

[9] Cf. Lorenzo D. Turner. 'The Impact of Western Education on the African's Way of Life', in *Africa Today* edited by C. Grove Haines (Baltimore, Johns Hopkins Press, 1955), pp. 154–155.
[10] In the Muslim areas, the schools for the sons of chiefs gave instruction in Koranic law and philosophy as well as a general French education.

to obtain an *aggrégation*, and that in *grammaire*, of which there are only five or six in France. Later, Senghor became a teacher in *lycées* at Tours and in Paris, and then at the Ecole Nationale de la France d'Outre-Mer, where he was appointed Professor of Negro-African Languages and Civilisation. He achieved distinction as both poet and essayist; besides numerous contributions to such periodicals as *Les Cahiers du Sud*, *Les Temps Modernes*, *Le Journal des Poètes*, his published works include *Chants d'Ombre*, *Hosties noires*, *Anthologie de la nouvelle poésie noire et malgache* and *Chants pour Noël éthiopiques*.

As the French sociologist Mercier has shown, the age-old grading of native societies into endogamous castes has produced a contemporary dichotomy into 'traditional' and 'modernist' élites. Thus prestige due to education may be superimposed on prestige deriving from tradition, and particularly from caste, as in the case of Félix Houphouët-Boigny who comes from a family of chiefs; or else the two may be completely separate. For even today a high standard due to personal achievement will not completely offset a traditional inferiority.[11]

Both Lord Hailey and Dietrich Westermann have denied that nationalism can have the same meaning in Africa as in Europe, namely a concept of territorial nationalism creating a desire for unity. Even in Europe such a concept has not always been uniformly applied. Alsace and the uncomfortable juxtaposition of different ethnic groups under one flag, characteristic of so many countries in central and eastern Europe, and even Belgium, are sufficient reminders of its imperfect application. Lord Hailey suggests the use of the term 'Africanism',[12] whilst Westermann writes that nationalism in Africa 'simply means independence from European domination. In Africa there are no nations, only

[11] Cf. D. Mercier, 'Evolution of Senegalese Elites', in *International Social Science Bulletin*, vol. VIII (1956) pp. 442–443.
[12] Hailey, pp. 251–252.

tribal groups.'[13] Even these have tended to become less compact in recent times, because of a territorial intermingling stimulated by the development of easy communications or, as in Senegal, the extension of groundnut cultivation to new areas.[14] What Professor Harlow has called 'resurgent tribalism' can thus best be analysed in terms of a protective reaction against the splintering of the tribal principle by rapid changes in inter-tribal economic relations.[15]

Whatever the term used, there is no doubt that the outcome of the Brazzaville Conference constituted a definite challenge to the aspirations of the articulate anti-colonialists who had expected a profound change in French thought as a result of the war. But the tone of the meeting was set by the announcement which appeared in the press a few days before the Conference opened:

Les fins de l'œuvre de civilisation accomplie par la France dans les colonies écartent toute idée d'autonomie, toute possibilité d'évolution hors du bloc français de l'Empire. La constitution éventuelle, même lointaine, de self-governments dans les colonies est à écarter.[16]

The Conference, 'which represented essentially the point of view of colonial administrators'[17] urged the granting of substantial administrative freedom to the French African territories, together with the maintenance of political unity. It recommended a federal constitution operating through a colonial or preferably a federal parliament, local Assemblies composed partly of Europeans and partly of Africans, and a federal authority whose powers should be clearly defined. Further recommendations were the abolition of the *indigénat* at the end of the war and the

[13] 'Cultural History of Negro Africa', in *Cahiers d'Histoire Mondiale*, vol. VII, no. 4 (1957), p. 1003.
[14] Cf. Mackenzie and Robinson, p. 285.
[15] Cf. 'Tribalism in Africa', in *Journal of African Administration*, vol. VII (1955) p. 17.
[16] Ernest Milcent, *L'A.O.F. entre en scène* (Paris, Bibliothèque de l'Homme d'Action, 1958) pp. 24–25.
[17] Kenneth Robinson, *The Public Law of Overseas France since the War* (Oxford, Institute of Colonial Studies, Reprint Series No. 1a, 1954). p. 7.

suppression of forced labour over a period of five years but with the proviso that a compulsory labour service should be established for men between the ages of twenty and twenty-five, exempted from military service.[18]

It was as a result of suggestions voiced at Brazzaville that the African territories were subsequently able to send representatives to Paris to take part in the first and second Constituent Assemblies in 1946. In the elections to the latter, de Gaulle's Provisional Government extended the suffrage to limited categories of non-citizens, though voters were divided into two separate colleges throughout tropical Africa, Madagascar and Algeria. But the time-honoured policy of centralised government and administration was not greatly changed by the establishment of the 'Union Française', the post-war name of the French Empire. The first draft Constitution for the Fourth Republic contained a number of far-reaching colonial reforms, the most significant of which was Article 41 which implied that the colonies would be free to choose their constitutional relationship with France. This draft was rejected in the referendum of 5 May 1946 and the liberal provision, which automatically lapsed, was not renewed until General de Gaulle's return to power in 1958. The decisions adopted by the second Constituent Assembly and accepted in the referendum of 13 October 1946 did not incorporate the Constitutional Committee's recommendations (based largely on a proposal submitted by one of the Algerian deputies, Ferhat Abbas)[19] that:

Les progrès que les peuples de l'union française accompliront avec le peuple français devront les conduire à la libre disposition

[18] Cf. René Pleven, 'The Political Transformation of the French Empire' in *The Colonial Review*, vol. VI; and *La Conférence Africaine Française, Brazzaville, 30 Janvier-8 Février 1944* (Paris, 1945) pp. 32–35.

[19] Ferhat Abbas was a member of the 'Groupe des Parlementaires d'Outre Mer' which propounded the most advanced proposals, such as the renunciation of French claims to sovereignty over colonial peoples and a period of twenty years within which each colonial territory might choose secession, federation or integration. See *Annexes aux procès-verbaux de la seconde Assemblée Constituante*. Articles 107–110.

d'eux-mêmes. Dans le cadre de l'union française, ils pourront choisir soit un statut d'Etat libre lié à la France par un traité international, soit une autonomie politique, soit une intégration complète à la République.[20]

Bidault's coalition Government set France on the unsteady course it was to follow in its relations with the Union, and later with the 'Communauté Française', until 1958—a course marked by its chronic inability to come down fully on the side of either independence or federation. On the one hand the Communists and Socialists[21] were pressing for generous reforms whilst, on the other, a vigorous campaign against the proposed reforms was conducted in the lobbies of the Palais Bourbon by European settlers and commercial interests through their organisation, the 'Etats Généraux de la Colonisation Française'. The ambivalence of French government policy led, as Professor Roger Pinto has pointed out,[22] to the tragic cycle of insurrection and war instigated by embittered nationalists overseas, once the enactment of the 1946 Constitution definitely precluded progressive and peaceful decolonisation. The plan for a Community which might have evoked an enthusiastic response from France's colonial peoples, who expected so much from the restored Republic, was replaced by a legalistic Union of the French Republic (declared 'indivisible')—which comprised France, the overseas departments and territories—and the associated territories and states.[23] In the A.O.F. there were eight 'overseas territories', which belonged to the 'Union Française' not in their own right but as constituent elements of the French Republic. Togo was an 'associated territory' not constitutionally part of the Republic.

[20] Charles-Henri Favrod, *L'Afrique seule* (Paris, Editions du Seuil, 1961), p. 20.
[21] The S.F.I.O. and the Communist Party were represented in the Bidault Government, together with Bidault's own Party, the M.R.P.
[22] Cf. *Le Monde*, 30 July 1950.
[23] Article 60 of the Constitution of the Fourth Republic.

The new Constitution's Article 72 stated that: 'Dans les territoires d'outre-mer, le pouvoir législatif appartient au Parlement en ce qui concerne la législation criminelle, le régime des libertés publiques et l'organisation politique et administrative.'

But the French Executive in practice continued to enjoy most of the powers to govern French African possessions that it had possessed before 1946, since Article 47 provided that the 'Président du Conseil des Ministres' might continue to issue decrees which did not conflict with existing legislation. The only parliamentary safeguard was that such decrees could be issued only after reference to the new consultative Assembly of the French Union.

The pivotal reform for France's overseas subjects was the 'French Edict of Caracalla',[24] the first 'loi Lamine Guèye' of 7 May[25] named after its author, the Senegalese deputy. This was restated as Article 80 of the 1946 Constitution. According to this, 'tous les ressortissants des territoires d'outre-mer ont la qualité de citoyen au même titre que les nationaux français de la métropole ou des territoires d'outre-mer'. As a result, the legal distinction which had made the inhabitants of the Senegalese *communes* privileged amongst the A.O.F.'s population, was swept away. The extension of citizenship did not, as did pre-war individual grants of citizenship, require the African inhabitants to accept the French 'Code civil', but only certain categories of the new citizens obtained the vote.[26] A revised penal code replaced the hated *indigénat* in the A.O.F., whilst the granting of 'republican liberties' to the overseas territories enabled Africans to create their own political organisations within a legal framework. Miscellaneous forms of

[24] Thomas Hodgkin, *Nationalism in Colonial Africa* (London, Frederick Muller, 1956) p. 36.
[25] Operative as from 1 June 1946.
[26] Cf. Kenneth Robinson, 'Constitutional Reform in French Tropical Africa', in *Political Studies*, vol. VI, no. 1, February 1958, p. 45.

compulsory labour, affecting the rural population, were simultaneously abolished.

Despite the recommendations of the Brazzaville Conference, the Union was not given a federal structure. The Constitution, although embodying elements from both the main tendencies of policy, was markedly weighted in favour of assimilation principles. New organs of government and representation were created, however: a President (the President of the Fourth Republic, *ex officio*); the 'Haut Conseil de l'Union Française' (composed of representatives of the French Government and of the Etats Associés), whose function was to assist the Government of the Republic in formulating policy for the Union; and the 'Assemblée de l'Union Française' (in which equal representation was granted to France and to all overseas possessions taken together), with 204 members, twenty-seven of them from the A.O.F. Yet this 'Assemblée' was only an emasculated version of the 'Colonial Parliament' or 'Federal Assembly' suggested at Brazzaville; Professor Robinson has described it as a 'body which epitomises the confusions and uncertainties of the constitution-making era'.[27] Its functions remained purely advisory and its powers were virtually confined to the right of being consulted on the text of decrees relating to the overseas territories (except those made in pursuance of Article 47).

The overseas territories were granted substantial representation in the metropolitan Parliament. Thus the A.O.F. was represented in the 'Assemblée Nationale' by twenty deputies[28] (out of 627), elected on the common roll, and in the 'Conseil de la République' by twenty senators (out of 320), elected by the 'Assemblées Territoriales' and by the deputies. These 'Assemblées Territoriales' (called 'Conseils

[27] Kenneth Robinson, *The Public Law of Overseas France since the War*, p. 19.
[28] This was the number definitely established in 1951, after the extension of the franchise.

Généraux' until 1952) were set up in each overseas Territory, and modelled on the 'Conseil Général' of a French département.   They were not legislative bodies; their principal powers were financial,[29] though they were consulted on many matters such as the drafts of local 'arrêtés', which constitute a form of delegated legislation.   Their membership varied between twenty and fifty until 1957. Separate electorates were established for the A.O.F.'s 'Assemblées Territoriales', except that of Senegal, where common-roll elections for the councils of the restored 'communes' continued to be the practice in spite of the fact that the Europeans, whose interests the system of separate electorates and representatives was devised to safeguard, were much more numerous in Senegal than in all the other territories of the A.O.F.[30] By 1956, there were 42,861 Europeans in Senegal and 82,210 in the whole of the A.O.F.[31]

At the federal level, the 'Grand Conseil' which met in Dakar was composed of forty members, five from each 'Assemblée Territoriale', indirectly elected by all the members voting together.   The new institution was concerned primarily with economic and financial matters and controlled the annual federal budget.   On the whole, it came to have less influence on the local administration than the 'Assemblées Territoriales', which were often able to influence its decisions despite their total lack of constitutional control.   In certain matters—such as cheap housing, public lands, poor relief, co-operatives, savings banks and litigation costs—they even possessed powers of decision, subject to approval by the 'Conseil d'Etat' in Paris which was also required to approve their decisions about territorial taxes

[29] Yet, like the French 'Conseils Généraux', they provided for 'obligatory expenses'.
[30] Cf. Mackenzie and Robinson, p. 292.
[31] Cf. *Annuaire Statistique de l'A.O.F.*, vol. V, tome 2 (Paris, 1957) pp. 173–175.

and loans (though in certain cases these were submitted to a minister).[32]

Considerable emphasis came to be placed on the economic and social implications of the granting of French citizenship to France's overseas subjects. Productivity had to be increased, standards of living improved and educational opportunities expanded if the full potentialities of their new status were to be realised. This led to a determined insistence on the expansion of public investment in an effort to transform the overseas territories into modern economic and social units. The main instrument for this was the 'Fonds d'Investissement pour le Développement Economique et Social de la France d'Outre-Mer' (usually known as F.I.D.E.S.), which was brought into being by a law of 30 April 1946[33]. The Fund was provided partly by annual subventions in the French budget, partly by contributions from the territories themselves and partly by long term loans granted to the Territories by the 'Caisse Centrale de la France d'Outre-Mer' (C.C.F.O.M.) at a rate of 1 per cent per annum. It was controlled by a Committee of Management presided over by the Minister of Overseas France, whose responsibility it was to draw up ten-year development plans[34] for each Territory and to establish public corporations ('sociétés d'état') or joint undertakings ('sociétés mixtes') for the purpose. The C.C.F.O.M. was likewise authorised to provide capital for approved development projects.

The needs of the indigenous peoples were met on the basis of scheduled priorities. From 1947 to 1958 the total sum of $2,146,000,000 was appropriated and spent, of which 46 per cent went to the A.O.F.[35] France contributed over 2 per cent of its Gross National Product in the form of

[32] Cf. Kenneth Robinson, p. 24.
[33] But was replaced in 1959 by the *Fonds d'Aide et de Coopération.*
[34] Replaced in 1949 by four-year programmes.
[35] Cf. Stewart C. Easton, *The Twilight of European Colonialism* (London, Methuen, 1961), p. 349.

aid to its overseas territories. This contribution was about as much over a period of ten years as it had been from 1900 to 1945.[36]

Whilst debt service payments constituted a heavy burden on the territorial budgets, it is surprising that the French economy was sufficiently resilient, so soon after 1946, and in spite of the Fourth Republic's invariably unbalanced budgets, to provide such enormous sums. A decrease in development did occur between 1952 and 1954, however, and is thought to have been responsible for the wave of labour unrest and strikes which occurred in the A.O.F. in 1954 and 1955.[37] Public investment 'under the Development Plan fell from nearly £18 million in 1952–3 to a little over £10 million in 1953–4. Private investment is presumed to have dropped by about £2 million.'[38]

F.I.D.E.S. has been criticised for wastefulness, especially in the earlier years, and because the investments are said to have been made deliberately more beneficial to French private enterprise than to the native populations for whose benefit they were intended. And this despite the fact that private enterprise invested less than one fifth of the sums invested by the French taxpayer. Large public works redounding to the advantage of French industry were accorded priority over smaller, but more useful, schemes.

'L'Union française se meurt faute de choisir entre l'assimilation et le fédéralisme', declared Jacques Soustelle in the days before he became an *intégriste* Governor-General of Algeria, whilst Professor Robinson states that 'the period from 1946 to 1955 was marked by "immobilisme" in the constitutional position of French Overseas Territories perhaps even more than in domestic metropolitan politics'[39]. The latter is a somewhat anachronistic as well as an unfair

[36] Cf. Charles-Henri Favrod, p. 22 (footnote 2).
[37] Cf. *West Africa*, 26 March 1955.
[38] Hailey, p. 1340.
[39] Mackenzie and Robinson, p. 292.

judgement. The earlier Governments of the Fourth Republic could hardly be expected—any more than the other régimes faced with equally intricate colonial problems—to have been either willing or able, each year, to grant fundamental constitutional reforms affecting overseas possessions.

Certain not unimportant reforms were in fact introduced by legislation during the decade. In 1947 a new category of local citizens, all African natives literate in French or Arabic, were entitled to the vote. In 1951, the franchise was further extended in the elections to the 'Assemblée Nationale' to those local citizens who were 'chefs de ménage', civil or military pensioners or 'mères de deux enfants vivants ou morts pour la France'. Thus the electorate, which had been 1,362,763 in 1946, rose to 5,061,025 for the 1951 elections. In 1952, the electorate for the 'Assemblées Territoriales' was likewise enlarged by dispensing with the requirement that 'chefs du ménage' should pay tax; Togo was granted the privilege of holding elections on a common roll as in Senegal.[40]

Since the very terms of the constitution precluded any public discussion of the fundamental colonial issue—that of independence—African political leaders at first chose to concentrate their efforts on the obvious inequalities between metropolitan and local citizens, the latter of whom remained virtually 'second-class citizens'. The second 'loi Lamine Guèye' of 1950 secured for African higher civil servants not only equal pay but also equal conditions of work, including holidays in France. Furthermore, as a result of political pressure from African trade-union leaders, helped in the lobbies of the 'Assemblée Nationale' by representatives of the French trade-union movement and reinforced with timely strike action, the 1952 'Code du Travail' granted many of the claims for minimum wage standards, shorter working hours, family allowances,

[40] Cf. *L'Année Politique*, 1952, pp. 427–431.

holidays with pay and collective bargaining rights.[41] 'Both these laws have had important long-term consequences. They have accustomed senior African civil servants to receive unusually high remuneration, and organised workers to expect the major employer, Government, to meet their wage demands when backed by the pressure of the trade union movement.'[42]

Finally, the local government reform of 1955 established forty-four 'full municipalities' throughout French tropical Africa, similar to the three already set up in Senegal. Elections to the new councils were held on a common roll, though a geographical delimitation of wards on an ethnic basis was permitted where appropriate in order to ensure minimum European representation.[43]

[41] Cf. P. Huguet, *Code du travail d'outre-mer: texte et commentaire* (Paris, Recueil Sirey, 1953); and P. Rivière, 'Labour Code for French African Territories' in the *International Labour Review*, LXVIII, 3, September 1953.
[42] Hodgkin and Schachter, pp. 397–398.
[43] Cf. Kenneth Robinson, 'Local Government Reform in French Tropical Africa' in the *Journal of African Administration*, vol. VIII, no. 4 (1956) pp. 179–185.

IV THE GROWTH OF PARTIES

THE ten years between the Constitution of 1946 and the adoption of the 'loi cadre' in 1956 witnessed a major development in French-speaking West Africa—the formation and crystallisation of African political parties.

Like most contemporary African political parties, those of the A.O.F. were products of the post-war period,[1] and like other African parties, they have proved to be very much more fluid than Western European or North American parties, since they operate in a complex social context which is constantly being modified. This accounts for the phenomenon which Mr. Michael Crowder has pleasantly summarised: 'In West Africa many political parties are born. Few survive into early childhood.'[2] The formation of parties is usually effected in an informal way: candidates stand as individuals, and then get together with other deputies with whom they provisionally agree on a common policy in order to form a loose parliamentary group, which immediately assumes the name of a political party.

The legislation of 1946, which enabled African political leaders for the first time to concentrate on developing legal parties, and which required African participation in French institutions and parliamentary procedures, constituted the framework within which the new politically conscious élite had to operate in the following decade. From their inception, the main French West African political parties presented an unusual feature: they developed in both a territorial and an inter-territorial context. This was perhaps a natural consequence of the establishment of elections for both the 'Assemblée Nationale' in Paris and

[1] Only one or two African parties, such as the Tunisian Néo-Destour, can trace a continuous history back to the early thirties.
[2] Michael Crowder, *Pagans and Politicians* (London, Hutchinson, 1959), p. 37.

the local 'Assemblées Territoriales' on a territorial basis
and of the simultaneous creation of a federal 'Grand
Conseil' which stimulated co-operation across territorial
boundaries.   This alternating polarisation produced a
complicated web of political allegiances which the new
dispensation written into the constitution of the Fifth
Republic in 1958 did not succeed uniformly in destroying.

Although the 1946 Constitution was bitterly criticised by
the deputies in the 'Assemblée Nationale' returned by
African electorates, it was impossible for African political
leaders in the A.O.F. openly to discuss the issue of independence if they wished their party to remain legal. The ruthless
repression of the Madagascar rebellion of 1947 made the
French authorities' attitude on the subject unmistakably
clear.   Therefore any belief in African self-government
expressed an attitude of mind but not a programme of
action.   At the same time it was altogether impossible for
any of the parties, however conservative, to pursue a policy
of unquestioning collaboration with the French administration, for this would have been tantamount to political
suicide. [3]

The most decisive factors in the formation of the A.O.F.'s
political parties were the granting of a sufficiently substantial
measure of power to local assemblies; the opportunity
provided by the representation of Africans in the 'Assemblée
Nationale' in Paris to encourage nationalist politicians to
come together; and the introduction of institutions and
procedures—such as an electoral system—which made it
possible for parties to operate with effect on the sovereign
power. Electoral systems not only stimulated the growth
of parties; they also provided African leaders with much-
needed experience of the handling of political issues, of mass
psychology and of the way in which the modern state's

[3] Though some parties—the 'Union Progressiste Mauritanienne', the
'Bloc Africain de Guinée', the 'Parti Togolais du Progrès' and the
'Union des Chefs et des Populations du Nord Togo'—came to be known
as 'partis de l'administration'.

power can be used to further or to jeopardise its citizens' interests. As Dr. Ruth Schachter has noted, 'elections synchronised political development among territories where political pressure was unequal. For example, Mauritania, Niger and some parts of Haute-Volta could have been, and in some respects were, ruled in the old paternal way for another few years after 1954.' Whereas in territories such as Senegal, Guinea, the Ivory Coast and Dahomey, elections constituted one of the most vital precipitants of political development on an organised and modern basis, in most of the northern belt, from Mauritania to Niger, the initial impetus provided by elections was to 'encourage the formation of small electoral groups, aiming at little else than filling the relatively lucrative new offices'.[4]

To promote the creation of African parties it was also necessary for new social groups to come into being whose common aspirations, since they could not be fulfilled without a significant devolution of sovereignty by the French State, would impel their most articulate representatives to strive for access to political power. Assomé Seck's statement that 'the class struggle shows itself, not in the relationships between class and the African mass, but in the relationships between the whole body of Africans and Europeans'[5] is a subtle analysis of the dynamics which transformed the power structure in African societies. For, although the new élites in Africa are often equated with an emergent middle class, the new social groups, whose concentration in the fast-developing urban agglomerations provided the future nucleus of the mass parties, in fact range from professionals, civil servants, entrepreneurs and planters,[6] to clerks, traders and wage-earners.

[4] Ruth Schachter 'The Development of Political Parties in French West Africa' (Unpublished Oxford doctoral thesis, 1958), quoted by Thomas Hodgkin, *African Political Parties* (Harmondsworth, Penguin Books, 1961) p. 38.

[5] Cf. INCIDI., 'Middle Classes in Tropical and Subtropical Countries' (Brussels, 1956). Record of the XXIXth Session.

[6] More particularly in the Ivory Coast.

The African-controlled popular press contributed to the rise of parties. But the lower literacy rate, stricter censorship and the requirement, up to 1945, that organs of the press should be directed by French citizens, made it a more hazardous enterprise than in the neighbouring British territories. Most newspapers in the A.O.F. had a very short life, as Amon d'Aby emphasised when listing and describing those appearing in the Ivory Coast before 1939:

On les voit naître, mais on ne sait jamais quand ni comment ils disparaissent. Leur existence dure de six mois à un an; les mieux soutenus ne dépassent guère trois ans, encore ce temps est-il coupé de longues périodes d'interruption. Le tirage des journaux varie de mille à deux mille cinq cents exemplaires.[7]

Writing of *L'Eclaireur de la Côte d'Ivoire*, the first newspaper in the colony to be founded and edited by local publicists, Amon d'Aby stated:

Le journal connut un succès immense dans le milieu africain. Il mena campagne contre les chefs supérieurs et les gardes de cercle, réclama le développement des oeuvres sociales, plaida en faveur des chômeurs et des planteurs indigènes frappés par la crise économique.[8]

But the life-span of this enterprising newspaper was from May to October 1935, though it was started up again in January 1936 by an 'originaire' of Saint-Louis du Sénégal.

However short-lived each newspaper may have been, the cumulative effect of a popular African press was considerable. It quickened the pace of what Dr. Azikiwe of Nigeria has called 'mental emancipation', whereby a people influenced by colonial symbols and shibboleths is offered an alternative set of 'nationalist' symbols and shibboleths. An African press managed to relate specific grievances of particular groups and areas to a coherent set of anti-colonialist doctrines, thereby stimulating the political consciousness and 'nationalist' awareness leading to action. Léopold Sédar Senghor's *Condition humaine*, 1948–1949, had

[7] F. J. Amon d'Aby, p. 62.
[8] Ibid., p. 64.

an even more direct influence, for it helped condition the thought and purpose of those who founded the 'Bloc Démocratique Sénégalais'.

Until 1945, French policy regarding freedom of association, speech and the press in its overseas possessions did not allow for political activity in the A.O.F. outside Senegal. The early proto-nationalist organisations of the African élite on the west coast of Africa and of the European residents in Dakar could only qualify as pressure groups. Such was the Senegalese branch of the 'Section Française de l'Internationale Ouvrière' (S.F.I.O.) formed by a group of opposition Socialists in the days of Blum's Popular Front Government. It was known as the 'Fédération Sénégalaise'. A political discussion group called the 'Foyer du Soudan' was formed at Bamako in 1937.

Although there existed throughout the A.O.F. 'an array of *amicales*, veterans' organisations, sports clubs, and youth groups, none of these could have been called a "party", and virtually none of them had any political orientation'.[9] When they *did* develop, tropical Africa's political parties presented certain features which distinguished them from the parties formed in British West Africa. The integrationist policy of the 'Union Française' proved far less favourable to the development of the spirit of territorial nationalism than did Britain's policy of colonial rule. Most of the parties which sprang up as a result of the post-war easing of controls, were ethnic or territorial. Others were offshoots of metropolitan parties, whilst only two—the 'Rassemblement Démocratique Africain' (R.D.A.) in 1946 and the 'Indépendants d'Outre-Mer' (I.O.M.) in 1947—developed organisations extending beyond the A.O.F.'s frontiers. Yet both these groups, as well as the socialists whose main party, the 'Bloc Démocratique Sénégalais' (B.D.S.) founded in 1948, was affiliated to the S.F.I.O., failed in their successive attempts to lead a 'Pan-French-African' movement.

[9] Thompson and Adloff, p. 83.

But the R.D.A. and the I.O.M. did succeed in developing links between African groups on a wide, inter-territorial basis. The measure of their success is the anger with which so many of the African political leaders greeted the 'loi-cadre', in 1956, when they denounced it as a plan for the 'balkanisation' of French tropical Africa.

What Thomas Hodgkin has described as the 'metro-politan axis' of political reference, has had very important implications for party development in the A.O.F. as else-where in the Union. African deputies and senators partici-pated in the work and responsibilities of the 'Assemblée Nationale'; this constituted the most valuable political right possessed by Africans. Not only did the 1946 Constitu-tion enable the African-elected representatives to prove how well they could handle the French language[10] and master the established parliamentary procedure; it also led them to develop an intensified consciousness of the community of African interests. Such a realisation only made the strong centralist and unitarian character of the French adminis-trative and political system appear more irksome, though some very close-working relationships between African and French political leaders and parties were established as a result of the constitutional nexus. Such relationships and the resulting interactions were a powerful stimulus in the actual formation of strong, cohesive African parties evolving from pressure groups. Referring to the cordial welcome extended to African parliamentary representatives in France, Momo Touré of Guinea compared some of the French politicians to the Minotaur as they seemed so 'friands de nègres'.[11]

Similarly, African deputies often influenced, quite considerably, the balance of force in the 'Assemblée Nationale'. Their power in the floating vote could even be compared, *mutatis mutandis*, to the part played in British

[10] This placed many of the traditional chiefs who were illiterate at an obvious disadvantage.

[11] Assemblée de l'Union Française debate, 12 February 1948.

politics by the 'Irish vote' during the second half of the nine-teenth century. These deputies either became affiliated, individually or as an African party, to one of the French parties or they formally joined French parties, and even became prominent in the leadership hierarchy. Conversely, French party leaders sought increased parliamentary strength by forming alliances with the African deputies and, more significantly, by organising party branches in the A.O.F. and running party candidates in African territorial elections.[12]

Whereas in the British tradition of parliamentary government the political party is regarded as 'a positive instrument for the integration of diverse interests, the formulation of public policy, and the provision of leadership that ultimately becomes the Government of the day'—and political parties with this object in view emerged in British West Africa as a result of the very substantial constitutional reforms effected between 1950 and 1953—the leaders of African political parties in the A.O.F. could not expect to receive 'what is normally conceived as the *raison d'être* of political parties—the meaningful exercise of executive power'.[13] Another factor which fashioned the special pattern of party development in French tropical Africa was the greatly increased post-war immigration of Europeans, particularly noticeable in such territories as Senegal, Soudan, the Ivory Coast, Guinea, Cameroun and Tchad. This did not involve a land-rush, however, since French theory reproduced the Dutch distinction between free state property which could be alienated and unfree state property belonging inalienably to the indigenous population, in accordance with prevailing native law. Thus Europeans were given right of entry only to the 'terres vacantes et

---

[12] The S.F.I.O. had established a section in Senegal as early as 1928 to win the seat of its deputy.
[13] James S. Coleman, 'The Emergence of African Political Parties', *Africa Today*, p. 246.

sans maître', while the tests of what constituted vacancy became ever stricter.[14]

All colonial powers practised some form of assimilationist policy, to a greater or lesser degree, but its most successful outcome—nationalism modelled on European patterns—was certainly not fostered by these powers. Yet African nationalism is 'the inevitable end-product of the impact of Western imperialism and modernity upon African societies; it is also the inevitable assertion by the Africans of their desire to shape their own destinies'.[15]

With the sole exception of Lamine Guèye, none of the post-war African leaders had any previous connexion with French parties. From the first election, held in 1945, the new African deputies chose to align themselves with one of the three major metropolitan parties. Lamine Guèye, Léopold Sédar Senghor and Yacine Diallo of Guinea, became *apparentés* to the S.F.I.O.; Houphouët-Boigny, Apithy of Dahomey and Sissoko of Soudan to the Communist Party; while some deputies from Cameroun joined forces with the M.R.P.

The 1946 Constitution provoked a hostile reaction among the new African leaders who considered its colonial provisions insufficiently liberal. The 'Groupe d'Etudes Communistes' at Dakar took advantage of this dissatisfaction and launched the idea of an African popular front, while Apithy,[16] a Socialist, stated in the Constituent Assembly that the African deputies' aim was not to sit 'sur les bords de la Seine, mais de traiter sur les bords du Congo-Niger les affaires de notre pays'.[17] A manifesto issued in September 1946 by five leading African deputies—Houphouët-Boigny, Sissoko, Tchicaya, Diallo and d'Arboussier—attacked the

[14] Cf. W. K. Hancock, *Survey of British Commonwealth Affairs* (London, Oxford University Press for the Royal Institute of International Affairs, 1942) vol. II, 'Problems of Economic Policy', Part 2, p. 179.
[15] James S. Coleman, 'Nationalism in Tropical Africa' in *American Political Science Review* (June 1954), p. 426.
[16] Apithy is the present Vice-President of Dahomey.
[17] Assemblée Constituante debate, 18 September 1946.

revival of colonialism implicit in the recently formed
'Etats Généraux de la Colonisation Française'[18] and urged
all African organisations seeking to achieve political and
economic democracy to hold an immediate congress at
Bamako.

As a result of a serious error of judgement, attributable to
the French Socialist Marius Moutet,[19] the African Socialist
deputies did not attend the Congress when it became clear
that they would not be able to dominate it as they had the
'Bloc Africain' formed in Senegal. Eight hundred delegates
from all parts of French black Africa, including the mandated territories, attended from 18 to 21 October. The new
'movement' created by the Congress under the name
'Rassemblement Démocratique Africain' was thus left to
ally itself with the French Communist Party which had
sent Raymond Barbé and other members in France to
Bamako. Although it posed as an African party, the R.D.A.
'used Communist techniques in organising mass meetings
and giving out slogans and party lines'.[20] There was no
organic relationship between the two parties, however,
though they maintained a parliamentary alliance until 1950.

The R.D.A. developed into an impressive organisation,
with sections throughout the A.O.F. (except Mauritania)
as well as in Middle Congo, Tchad and Cameroun. Its
stronghold was in the Ivory Coast, organised by the wealthy
Baulé planter and Ponty-trained doctor, Houphouët-
Boigny; it became the dominant mass party in Soudan,
under Mamadou Konaté,[21] and after 1955 in Guinea,
Cameroun and Tchad. To a lesser extent it also dominated
the political scene in Upper Volta, Niger and Middle
Congo, but remained a small party in Senegal and
Dahomey. It had its own journal, *Afrique Noire*.

[18] On 30 July 1946.
[19] Minister of Overseas France from January 1946 to October 1947.
[20] Thompson and Adloff, p. 85.
[21] Konaté died in 1956; thereafter the leadership passed to Modibo
Keita.

Each territorial 'section' was guided by a 'comité directeur', which co-ordinated the activities of the regional 'sous-sections' and local 'comités de quartier' and 'comités de village'. A 'comité de co-ordination' was in principle responsible for the R.D.A.'s inter-territorial control; in fact, however, links were maintained through the R.D.A. deputies in Paris. Only three inter-territorial congresses were held in Africa between 1946 and 1958.

Among the R.D.A.'s objectives were equality of political and social rights, local democratic assemblies, and a freely negotiated union of African peoples with France. Thousands of party cards, priced at about 100 francs C.F.A., were sold and it claimed to have 'millions of sympathisers' at the height of its influence.[22] By 1950, however, mounting criticism against the party's overt domination by French Communists—accompanied by the resignation of a large number of supporters—precipitated a crisis between the R.D.A.'s President, Houphouët-Boigny, and its mulatto Secretary-General, Gabriel d'Arboussier. D'Arboussier enjoyed a position of great influence, not only because of his management of the party but also because of his remarkable intellectual powers and political training. A militant Communist, he was opposed by Houphouët-Boigny who now favoured a policy of compromise with the French Administration after the failure of the R.D.A.-inspired outbreaks in the Ivory Coast, which led to the death of fifty-two Africans and to about 3,000 arrests. The R.D.A.'s right wing was left in control, while the left retained its influence in the expelled dissident 'sections' in Senegal and Cameroun, in the left wing of the Niger 'section' and among youth movements, students and trade unionists.[23]

An important split also occurred in the socialist 'Bloc Africain' of Senegal, where the young Catholic intellectual, Senghor, attacked the jobbery, nepotism and sectional policies associated with Lamine Guèye's leadership. In 1948

[22] Cf. Hodgkin, *Nationalism in Colonial Africa*, p. 166.
[23] Cf. *Afrique Noire*, 24 July 1952.

Senghor formed the 'Bloc Démocratique Sénégalais', with Mamadou Dia, a highly intelligent Muslim schoolteacher, as his second-in-command. Together they developed the new party's ideology, basing it on a new, specifically African form of socialism. While concentrating on practical demands—improved groundnut prices, democratic co-operatives, new schools and medical facilities—they urged the relevance of Negro-African values, such as emphasis upon the group, the 'collectivité', but within a context of increasing autonomy.[24]

On the other hand, a recognition of common national or regional interests often resulted in alliances between the old élite and the new; such was the merger in Upper Volta, in 1956, of the nationalist R.D.A. (under its local name of 'Parti Démocratique Voltaïque') and the traditionalist 'Parti Social d'Education des Masses Africaines'. Together they formed the 'Parti Démocratique Unifié' under the honorary presidency of Mogho Naba, hereditary ruler of the Mossi kingdom.

The economic grievances of the African planters, the cash-crop farmers cultivating cocoa and coffee, provided the main post-war political stimulus in the Ivory Coast. Before 1945, the French had encouraged Europeans to settle as planters there.[25] During the thirties, forced labour had supplied European estates with African workers, while under the Vichy régime Europeans' crops received higher prices and priority rights. The Ivory Coast thus provided an unusual phenomenon: an anti-colonial movement with predominently agrarian roots, organised through the 'Syndicat Agricole Africain'. The S.A.A., founded in 1944 by Houphouët-Boigny, transcended ethnic boundaries and established a network of local branches which campaigned against forced labour and recruited only voluntary workers. The organisation and finances of the 'Syndicat' formed the

[24] Cf. *Condition Humaine*, 25 February 1948.
[25] Cf. H. Frechon, *Les plantations européennes en Côte d'Ivoire*, (Dakar, Institut des Hautes Etudes, 1955).

basis of the 'Parti Démocratique de la Côte d'Ivoire', which later became the R.D.A.'s territorial 'section'. From 1946, the Ivory Coast 'established itself as a rival centre of political activity and locus of power to Senegal. At about this time it was above all the Ivory Coast which appeared to the French authorities to be charged with revolutionary possibilities.'[26]

The structure and programmes of the A.O.F.'s African parties were greatly influenced by Western political organisation and ideologies, but they also derived inspiration from both pre-colonial experience and their own existing, traditional patterns of authority. Thus the 'Parti Démocratique de Guinée' (the R.D.A.'s local 'section') stressed its connexions with Samory Touré's 'empire', while the 'Union Soudanaise' revived ideas which had characterised the 'empire' of Hajj' Umar al-Tal. The 'Union Progressiste Mauritanienne' merely reproduced 'the working alliances of the fief-holders, supported by their clients and vassals'.[27] The A.O.F. was fortunate in not being cursed with any prophet movements which might develop into parties based on messianic hopes such as impinged on the political scene in the Bakongo areas of both the A.E.F. and the Belgian Congo. But there are links between Muslim religious sects and some political groups in Senegal. On the other hand, tribal resurgence was an important generator of political organisation and claims. For example, the vigorous Ewe renaissance, stimulated by colonial partition was very largely instrumental in creating those parties striving for the unification of Togo and Togoland, namely the 'Comité de l'Unité Togolaise', JUVENTO and the Togoland congress.

As a result of its ubiquity, the quality of its leadership, the impact of its influence and the strength of the ties of loyalty which it created among its adherents, the R.D.A. was

26 Hodgkin and Schachter, p. 412.
27 Hodgkin, *African Political Parties*, p. 19.

until 1958 the most important inter-territorial political organisation in French tropical Africa. It served as a model for Patrice Lumumba's 'Mouvement National Congolais'.

The R.D.A.'s unity depended essentially on the relative stability of its competent leadership and on the policy of African emancipation which it consistently pursued. The special circumstances of its genesis had one far-reaching result. The voluntary withdrawal of the Socialists from Bamako led to Senegal's isolation from the vanguard of the A.O.F.'s anti-colonial movement. For twelve vital years the principal Socialist stronghold sought to create rival inter-territorial groupings, all of which failed to acquire any significance comparable to that of the R.D.A. They took the form of temporary alliances among territorial parties, but never developed the characteristics or prestige of a universally accepted popular movement. The satisfaction which the Socialists' discomfiture over such ventures gave to their political opponents was enhanced by the fact that the Socialists concerned were Senegalese. Africans from other territories had not yet forgiven the Senegalese their former enjoyment of special privileges in the Federation. Thus the 'Indépendants d'Outre-Mer', founded in 1947 by Senghor and Dr. Louis Ajoulat[28], deputy from Cameroun, included both French and indigenous parliamentarians from black Africa. Though its ranks were swelled by desertions from the R.D.A., after the 1949–50 insurrectionary outbreaks in the Ivory Coast, it was not until 1953, at its Congress at Bobo-Dioulasso, that it formulated a precise policy: the principle of African autonomy within a federal French Republic. A compromise maintaining the existing Union, and worked out by Mamadou Dia (later elected the I.O.M.'s General Secretary), was accepted provisionally, however, on condition that the effective

[28] His appointment as Under-Secretary for Overseas France in November 1949 brought the I.O.M. considerable prestige.

decentralisation advocated by Raphael Saller,[29] was carried out.

When trying to form a Government, after Mendès-France was overthrown early in 1955, Christian Pineau offered a portfolio to Fily Dabo Sissoko but excluded Senghor on the grounds that he was unacceptable to the French Socialists. Pineau failed to get the required majority of votes when he presented his team to the 'Assemblée Nationale', as the I.O.M. automatically refused its confidence. But the elections of January 1956 altered the I.O.M.'s position as a determining factor in the making and unmaking of French Governments. Ajoulat was defeated and the I.O.M.'s deputies were reduced to below the fourteen required to form an autonomous parliamentary bloc eligible for consultation by the President of the Republic before the formation of a new Government. The I.O.M. was succeeded in 1957 by the 'Convention Africaine' which, in turn, gave way by 1958 to the 'Parti de Regroupement Africain'. The P.R.A. united virtually all non-R.D.A. parties outside Mauritania, and attempted to effect a merger with the R.D.A. At its Cotonou congress, it stressed the need for independence, unity and inter-African solidarity in the struggle for African emancipation. Although they were unsuccessful, these short-lived political organisations were significant in that they symbolised Senghor's determination to offset the African Socialists' failure to participate in the A.O.F.'s only inter-territorial political movement.

After the A.O.F.'s territorial elections in March 1957 and the Togo elections of April 1958, mass parties predominated in the shape of the 'Union Progressiste Sénégalaise'[30] in Senegal, the P.D.C.I. in the Ivory Coast, the P.D.G. in

[29] Saller, though a Frenchman, is at present the Ivory Coast's 'Ministre des Finances, des Affaires Economiques et du Plan'.
[30] Made up of Senghor's 'Bloc Populaire Sénégalais' (the Bloc Démocratique Sénégalais's new name since 1956) and of Lamine Guèye's Socialists, who had finally broken their twenty-year-old connexion with the S.F.I.O. in Paris.

Guinea, the 'Union Soudanaise' in Soudan and the 'Comité de l'Unité Togolaise' (C.U.T.) in Togo. The same tendency to mass parties, though on a smaller scale, was apparent in Niger, Upper Volta and Dahomey. Only in Mauritania, controlled by a semi-military French administration, did a 'parti de l'administration' (the 'Union Progressiste Mauritanienne') survive.

V THE FRENCH COMMUNITY: MIRAGE OR REALITY

Part I The 'Loi Cadre'

IN 1956 the political climate in the French Union enabled independence to become a live issue in the A.O.F. African leaders had built powerful mass parties and had developed trade unions and youth movements in the Ivory Coast, Senegal, Guinea and Soudan. The instability of French Governments, France's humiliation at Dien-Bien-Phu, her surrender to the forces of nationalism in Tunisia and Morocco, and her embroilment in Algeria, all led to vacillation and compromise in the face of African demands. Such demands were given body by the 1955 reforms in Togo, which came nearer than anything so far to an accept-ance of the principle of self-government. The elections to the 'Assemblée Nationale' in 1956 demonstrated the strength of moderate nationalism in the French African territories. It was clearly time to redefine their relationships with the metropolitan country. The attitude of Guy Mollet's Socialist Government was summarised in the 'exposé des motifs' appended to the Bill which was introduced in February of that year and which prescribed general lines of reform while leaving details to be settled by decree:

Il ne faut pas se laisser devancer et dominer par les événements pour ensuite céder aux revendications lorsqu'elles s'expriment sous une forme violente. Il importe de prendre en temps utile les dispositions qui permettront d'éviter les conflits graves.[1]

The 'loi cadre' was finally enacted in June 1956. It laid down the general principles for a revision of the relation-ships between France and the African territories; it granted new legislative powers in specific spheres, such as soil

[1] Quoted by Kenneth Robinson, 'Constitutional Reform in French Tropical Africa', *Political Studies*, vol. VI, no. 1, February 1958, p. 48.

conservation and internal trade and it abolished the system of separate electorates; it established universal suffrage on a common roll in all elections.

The most important of the reforms concerned the very structure of government: the powers of the 'Gouvernement-Général' were reduced and 'Conseils de Gouvernement' were to be established for each Territory. These executives, elected by the 'Assemblées Territoriales', were to be predominantly African, but to contain a number of French officials.[2] The French territorial Governor was to remain in control of the 'state' services, to possess certain reserved powers and to preside over the 'Conseil de Gouvernement'.

The Minister for Overseas France, who was responsible for introducing the 'loi cadre' was the Socialist Deputy and Mayor of Marseille, Gaston Defferre, described as 'un des rares parlementaires français qui ose regarder les réalités en face et qui s'efforce de vivre avec son temps'.[3] The projet Defferre', as it was commonly dubbed, was carried by 477 votes to 99 in the 'Assemblée Nationale' and by 154 to 63 in the 'Conseil de la République'. It sought to bring about administrative decentralisation in the A.O.F. and to develop territorial autonomy. The federal power was no longer conceived of as an organ of direct governmental control, but as an instrument of co-ordination 'in terms of devolution within a unitary system, though admittedly a political and not merely an administrative devolution'.[4]

If the 'loi cadre' provoked scepticism in the A.O.F., the subsequent decrees—more than forty-five in number— caused dissatisfaction throughout the Federation, where they were derisively described as 'des joujoux ou des sucettes'.[5] African opinion was divided over the fundamental issue of how best to reconstitute the federal structure. The Senegalese parliamentarians were alone in demanding

[2] In practice, the 'Conseils de Gouvernement' contained no official other than the Governor.
[3] Ernest Milcent, p. 114.
[4] Robinson, *Constitutional Reform in French Tropical Africa*, p. 62.
[5] Ernest Milcent, p. 116.

a federal executive. Their views were consequently never taken into consideration by the 'Assemblée Nationale' in spite of the A.O.F.'s 'Grand Conseil' which upheld the Senegalese view. The French Government was no doubt swayed by Houphouët-Boigny who, as Mollet's 'Ministre Délégué à la Présidence du Conseil', was the first African accorded a French Cabinet position and who was wedded to the principle of the individual association of African territories with France.

The 'loi cadre's' most eloquent critic was Léopold Sédar Senghor who, in February 1957, in an interview with *Le Monde's* correspondent in Dakar stated:

Nous estimons que préconiser l'autonomie des territoires, c'est ne pas vouloir cette autonomie. En effet les 'Européens' pensent que 43 millions de Français ne peuvent résoudre les grands problèmes politiques et économiques qui se posent en 1957. Comment 3 millions de Soudanais ou simplement 600,000 Mauritaniens le pourraient-ils? Dans le cadre d'une république fédérale française, une A.O.F. de 20 millions d'habitants en face de la métropole peut constituer un ensemble équilibré et faire épanouir sa personnalité. Une Côte d'Ivoire ou un Sénégal de 2 millions d'habitants ne le peuvent pas. C'est pourquoi nous considérons que la loi cadre est une régression dans la mesure où elle balkanise les fédérations d'Afrique Noire. Cependant cette loi cadre peut être un instrument d'émancipation si les Africains le veulent.[6]

The political implications provoked fierce criticism. The editor of *L'Etudiant d'Afrique Noire*,[7] Albert Tevoedjre of Dahomey, stated that the 'loi cadre' might result in a multiplicity of small autonomous states 'entre lesquels le Gouvernement français—arbitre paternel—maniera ads-mirablement l'arme de la flatterie, du régionalisme et . . . de la différenciation économique',[8] and dismissed it as 'un

---

[6] *Le Monde*, 2 February 1957.
[7] Published in Paris as the monthly journal of the 'Fédération des Etudiants d'Afrique Noire en France'.
[8] Albert Tevoedjre, *L'Afrique revoltée* (Paris, Présence Africaine, 1958) p. 26.

modeste aménagement du système colonial'.[9]   At one
stroke, the French Government had destroyed France's
greatest contribution to tropical Africa: federal unity, with
freedom of movement for all, irrespective of origin. What
was impugned at Bamako as 'racisme interne' led to the
exacerbation of a form of territorial nationalism that was as
arbitrary in its origins as it has proved ruinous in its
administrative consequences. There are now 160 Ministers
and Secretaries of State, with a retinue of 'chefs' or 'direct-
eurs de cabinet', technical advisers, attachés and heads of
mission abroad, for fourteen French-speaking States with
30 million inhabitants. Mollet's Government was accused
of acting out of political self-interest in dismembering the
A.O.F. and the A.E.F. A proliferation of parties would
obviously facilitate a policy of 'divide and rule'. French
colonial administrators were suspected of urging Defferre
to enact the 'loi cadre' in order to maintain their position as
'les premiers en Province, plutôt que les seconds à Rome'.[10]
French private interests were held responsible for what was
interpreted as an attempt to secure a firmer capitalist hold
on the African economy by splitting the Federation.

The 'loi cadre' was a tacit recognition of the fact that the
1946 Constitution was no longer acceptable to responsible
Africans. The reforms divided the 'indivisible Republic'
and distributed power between France and its African
Territories, and fuller constitutional revision was bound to
follow, for the 'loi cadre' was but one stage in the now
inevitable decolonisation process. The old assimilationist
principle had been swept away and the ground prepared for
a new association.

But what form was this new association to take? Constitutional revision was discussed actively at official and
unofficial levels after 1956 and by the spring of 1958 the
second stage in decolonisation was being studied and

[9] Ibid., p. 142.
[10] Africanus, *L'Afrique noire devant l'indépendance* (Paris, Plon, 1958) p. 76.

planned. This involved tackling the very problems which General de Gaulle, after his return to power in May, sought to solve through the creation of a unit—part federal, part confederal—known as the 'Communauté Française'.

Both French and African leaders stressed the inadequacy of the 'Union', whose 'Conseil' had always lacked leverage on the decisions of the Government and the 'Assemblée Nationale'. The 'Conseil's' discussions had seldom aroused any public interest, while its influence on French colonial policy had been negligible. African deputies were able to make a decisive impact on the 'Assemblée Nationale' only when French parties were in a precarious balance. They rarely held Cabinet positions: Houphouët-Boigny, who held Cabinet rank uninterruptedly from February 1956 to May 1959, was exceptional.[11]

Although the 'loi cadre' and the decrees of 1957 enabled Frenchmen to cling to the distinction, however illusory, between local administrative autonomy and political independence, the balkanisation of the A.O.F. split African leadership along lines which foreshadowed the disintegration of the R.D.A. after the Referendum of 1958. While prevarication and evasion were the marks of French policy, time worked against a viable Franco-African relationship acceptable to Africans.[12]

The crisis occasioned by the 'loi cadre' turned on the related issues of independence and federalism and led to the third R.D.A. Congress, held at Bamako, in September 1957. Houphouët-Boigny, who advocated territorial autonomy within a federal French-African Community, was openly challenged by the powerful 'sections' of Guinea and Soudan, who emphasised the need for preserving the Federation's unity, in order to facilitate the rapid achievement of full independence.

[11] After breaking with the Communists in 1950, Houphouët-Boigny and the R.D.A. had allied themselves with the U.D.S.R. (Union Démocratique et Socialiste de la Résistance).

[12] Cf. Edgar S. Furniss, Jr., France—Troubled Ally (London, Oxford University Press, for the Council on Foreign Relations, 1960), p. 190.

Part 2   The Rise of Sékou Touré

By the end of 1957, Guinea had become the A.O.F.'s most dangerous powder-keg. Her conservative post-war leader, a schoolteacher named Yacine Diallo, together with another schoolmaster, Mamba Somo and a Muslim of mixed parentage, Maurice Monrat, gave Guinea eight years of political progress. But two events occurred in 1954 which completely revolutionised the territory's hitherto orthodox though unspectacular development. The first was Diallo's death and the second the soaring growth of the mining industry which, almost overnight, created a proletariat freed from the restraints of an African tribal society. This combination of circumstances proved favourable to one of Diallo's opponents, Sékou Touré, who was determined to seize political leadership. As a result of so doing, Sékou Touré developed an African personality able to rival Nkrumah as a cynosure.

Sékou Touré was born at Faranah in 1922 and despite his claim to kinsmanship with Samory came of poor peasant stock. He had a primary education and was later expelled from a trade school for organising a food strike. He was employed in 1940 by the Compagnie du Niger Français, a subsidiary of Unilever Ltd., but a year later he became a post office clerk.[13] He rose to power in Guinea as a labour organiser who quickly set himself apart from others by his remarkable capacity for work. His activities took such a radical tinge that the Governor arranged to have him transferred to the Ivory Coast's colonial service, but he refused to leave Guinea. Elected General Secretary of the 'Syndicat des Transmissions de Guinée', in 1944, he rose to hold the office of General Secretary of the 'Union des Syndicats' *de Guinée*, from 1947 to 1956, while also being General Secretary of the 'Parti Démocratique de Guinée' (P.D.G.-R.D.A.) from 1948 to 1957.

[13] For a description of the *Compagnie du Niger Français*, cf. Jean and René Charbonneau, *Marchés et marchands d'Afrique noire* (Paris, La Colombe, 1961) pp. 70–71.

In 1956, Sékou Touré became President of the 'Confédération Générale des Travailleurs Africains' which he had founded together with some colleagues in the French C.G.T. The new organisation was to be an autonomous group with no affiliations with either the metropolitan (and Communist) body or the W.F.T.U. This development followed the R.D.A.'s electoral victory in January 1956 and paralleled the A.O.F.'s political evolution.[14]

A conference of delegates from the trade union movement in French black Africa met at Cotonou, in January 1957, to unite and organise the workers as well as 'affirm the personality of African trade unionism'.[15] Its most important achievement was the formation of an independent 'Union Générale des Travailleurs de l'Afrique Noire', of which Sékou Touré remained President until January 1959. UGTAN received the French authorities' blessing, notably that of the Haut-Commissaire[16] Cornut-Gentille, who realised that it would seriously weaken the C.G.T.'s influence. The trade-union leadership trained in Marxist thought and methods and of which Sékou Touré became the foremost figure, impressed definite characteristics upon the P.D.G. during the crucial years 1953 to 1957 when it established itself as Guinea's dominant party. Although its ideas were derived from the R.D.A., the P.D.G. directed its main propaganda to the underprivileged and claimed to be the organised expression of the popular will.

In the 1954 election, Touré opposed Barry Diawadou, Diallo's political heir. There can be little doubt that the election was rigged by the administration, and there was violent protest when Diawadou was declared—after a significant delay—the victor. Observers at the polls maintained that Sékou Touré had scored a resounding victory. The defeat of the conservative ex-colonial governor Raphaël Saller in the 1955 senatorial election was another

[14] Cf. Thompson and Adloff, pp. 506–507.
[15] Ibid., p. 509.
[16] As the Governor-General was now termed.

indication of the new political trend in Guinea. Elections continued to be marked by outbreaks of violence which was no longer limited to Conakry, but spread to Macenta and Boké.

Most Europeans remained aloof, but in November 1955, when Touré was elected Mayor of Conakry, a few reactionary white settlers launched an organisation, 'Présence Française', modelled on the extremist settler group in Algeria. In the following year, the extreme left European element joined the R.D.A. and described the recurrent outbreaks in Conakry as manifestations of an oppressed proletariat rising up against an African bourgeoisie in the colonialists' pay.[17]

Far less imbued with French culture than the A.O.F.'s other outstanding leaders, Sékou Touré went to Paris as Guinea's Deputy in 1956. He had already visited Paris, as a trade union delegate, in 1946 and 1950. During his first stay, he had joined the Socialists, attending the 'conférences de cadres' given by Tollet and Dufriche or listening to Pierre Hervé's 'exposés politiques'. Later, he went to Czechoslovakia. The precise date of this visit is not known, for so far Touré has maintained silence about it. What is certain, however, is that he attended the 1950 Warsaw Peace Congress.[18] In Paris, he shared a studio flat near the Hôtel de Ville with Fodéba Keïta, founder of the 'ballets africains', who has since become his Minister of the Interior. He spent a lot of his time in Paris, assiduous in parliamentary attendance, but he spoke only six times in the 'Assemblée Nationale' from January 1956 to 1958—in marked contrast to the large number of speeches he made in Guinea. He was determined from the outset not to become a cog in the French political machine and invariably refused ministerial office in Paris.

Because of his unconcealed hostility to the 'loi cadre', he became bitterly opposed to Houphouët-Boigny. As early

[17] Thompson and Adloff, p. 138.
[18] Cf. Jean Lacouture, p. 329.

as March 1956, in a verbal duel with Defferre, Touré stated:

Il faudra d'abord affirmer que l'unité sera realisée, soit sur la base du statut de 1946, soit sur la base d'un statut nouveau, mais qui sera le même pour tous . . . Confier aux assemblées territoriales la charge de fixer les règles de la fonction publique, c'est les mettre dans une situation très difficile.[19]

When the 'loi cadre' was implemented in 1957, Sékou Touré was elected Vice-President of the 'Conseil de Gouvernement', while the P.D.G.-R.D.A. won fifty-six out of the sixty seats in the 'Assemblée Territoriale'. Touré had already set about destroying the last remnants of political opposition to the *parti unique* which the P.D.G. planned to be. The French Governor proved powerless to intervene when Touré and his henchmen resorted to the most violent methods of intimidation.

One of the first reforms introduced by Touré, in pursuit of a levelling policy, was the abolition of the office of 'chef de canton' and the substitution of regular civil servants advised by popularly elected 'conseils de conscription' and 'conseils de village'. At one blow, the P.D.G. neutralised the reactionary elements forming the core of the *chefferies*. Sékou Touré, who considered himself first and foremost an African, actively followed a policy of africanisation. His first Government, formed in May 1957, nevertheless included two Europeans.

Guinea became one of the outstanding examples of a type of African political system that Sékou Touré has called a 'démocratie populaire'. The governing party became identified with the State and all opposition was contained within it. The party—the P.D.G.—became virtually co-extensive with the entire citizen body. Special encouragement was given to women to join the party and women soon came to represent an important political force. Touré had

[19] Cf. Jean Lacouture, p. 334.

this to say of Guinea women in an interview granted to the Swiss journalist Fernand Gigon:

... ce sont surtout les femmes, pratiquement pas touchées par le régime colonial et pas associées aux organismes économiques ou administratifs de ce même régime, qui formaient l'appui essentiel de notre action. C'est d'elles que nous pouvions recevoir la force la plus dynamique parce qu'en elles l'ésperance dans le progrès était totale.[20]

Part 3 Birth of the Community

The French Referendum of September 1958 constituted a watershed in the political history of French-speaking West Africa. A transformation in the relationship between France and her overseas possessions was long overdue, and one of de Gaulle's first acts when he came to power was the creation of the French Community. But the idea of a French-African Community was an African, rather than a French, notion. At the 1957 Bamako conference, all parties and delegates—with the exception of a few young Africans impressed by the example of Ghana—had joined together to urge the French to create such a Community. Many African leaders believed that Africa had something to contribute to, as well as something to receive from, a purposeful relationship with France on a full partnership basis. Men like Senghor and Houphouët-Boigny considered that a French-African Community was something desirable in itself, in a world becoming increasingly nationalistic.

But fundamental differences of opinion became apparent at Bamako as soon as discussion centred on the form a French-African Community should take. The majority of the R.D.A. delegates[21] wanted to recreate the Federations and grant them fully responsible government, while leaving certain powers relating to foreign affairs, defence and economic policy in French hands. They advocated a

[20] Cf. Fernand Gigon, *Guinée etat-pilote* (Paris, Plon, 1959) p. 22.
[21] With the exception of the Mauritanians who, on account of their closer affinities with North Africans, displayed very little enthusiasm for the creation of a federal French West African state ruled by Africans.

federal Chief Executive and a Cabinet with limited powers (to replace the 'Grand Conseil') responsible to a federal Parliament in both West and Equatorial Africa. This would result in two large and potentially viable self-governing units under responsible Africans sharing certain well-defined responsibilities with France. They insisted that Africans should enjoy a measure of control over the allocation of French subsidies and public investment funds, in return for their willingness to guarantee the safety of all foreign investments, private and public. It was felt that such self-governing States would be capable of playing an effective role in a federal entity comprising France and all its overseas possessions.

A minority opinion in the R.D.A. was held by its President, by a solid bloc of Ivory Coast delegates and by Léon Mba, Vice-President of Gabon, the A.E.F.'s richest territory. Houphouët-Boigny proposed that each Territory should be autonomous and that the whole of Overseas France should then enter, as units, into equal relationship to the French Republic. Certain powers should be reserved to the Federal Executive, while each Territory should be directly represented in the federal institutions in Paris. Such a conception was basically particularist in that it predicated territorial but not federal autonomy; it was Houphouët-Boigny's view that the 'Grands Conseils' of the Federations should be abolished. He was confident that a federal government, including Africans and Frenchmen, would take full account of African interests. Appointments would be made on grounds of merit and not of race: had he himself not been appointed recently French Minister of Health?

Senghor likewise believed in a true federal republic, but maintained that the A.O.F.'s Territories should be grouped together to strengthen their influence. Both he and Houphouët-Boigny sincerely regarded the federal Community as a desirable end in itself and not merely as a transitional stage in the dialectical process towards full sovereignty. But this ideal was never accepted by Sékou

Touré, although he regarded continued co-operation with France as an economic necessity. Because he desired the completion of the major industrial and constitutional projects which France had planned in Guinea, Touré was prepared to postpone independence, but not to forego it by becoming absorbed into a larger political unit which could never be fully controlled by Africans.

The official resolution of the Bamako conference concealed these fundamental differences of opinion, and because of Houphouët-Boigny's prestige and influence it was the minority view that prevailed. This fact alone is of the utmost significance in understanding the rapid failure to which the Gaullist conception of the French Community was doomed.

It was incumbent upon de Gaulle's régime to convince the African élites that it would press forward where its predecessor had prevaricated. Speed was indeed essential since such leaders as Modibo Keïta of Soudan doubted whether France would respond adequately. Keïta, the future President of Mali, had uttered a warning in March 1958 when still a member of Félix Gaillard's Government, that if France failed to create a French-African Community, Africans would inevitably seek full independence.[22] In view of this mistrust, de Gaulle entrusted the task of drawing up the new Constitution to his Cabinet instead of to the weakened 'Assemblée'. The need for swift action also accounts for de Gaulle's decision to allow the inhabitants of the overseas territories to participate in the constitutional referendum as fully as the citizens of France.

As conceived by de Gaulle and his 'Comité Consultatif Constitutionnel', the Community was made up of autonomous States. The constitutional draft referred to a 'Fédération' but, as the 'Comité Consultatif Constitutionnel' was divided between Federalists and Confederalists, with no

[22] Cf. Andre Blanchet, *L'Itinéraire des partis africains depuis Bamako* (Paris, Plon, 1958) pp. 147–148.

hope of compromise, it was decided to adopt the term Community.[23]

The Community was granted special powers in regard to foreign policy, defence, currency, common economic and financial policy, strategic raw materials and, 'sauf accord particulier', justice, higher education, transport and telecommunications.[24]

It was to have a President, who was also President of the French Republic, and he was to preside over a consultative 'Conseil Exécutif' comprising the heads of the member States[25] and 'les ministres chargés, par la Communauté, des affaires communes'.[26] A purely consultative 'Sénat', comprising representatives of the constituent legislatures,[27] and a 'Cour Arbitrale', whose composition and competence were to be established by an organic law,[28] completed the institutional structure.

The new Constitution was explicit on one major point. A change in the status of a member of the Community could be requested either by a Territory, through action taken by its legislature and confirmed by a referendum, or by the French Republic. Article 86 went on to say: 'Dans les mêmes conditions, un Etat membre de la Communauté peut devenir indépendant. Il cesse de ce fait d'appartenir à la Communauté.' In view of de Gaulle's later reactions to such problems as Guinea's secession, it would seem fair to say that his Government offered autonomy to the African Territories as an alternative to full independence, rather than as a step towards it. The French probably assumed that independence would be less attractive to leaders of financially dependent States of approximately three million

[23] Cf. *Notes et Etudes Documentaires No. 2.* 530, 11 avril 1959 (Paris, La Documentation Française) p. 30.
[24] Constitution du 4 Octobre 1958, Titre XII, Article 78.
[25] In addition to the A.O.F. States, the Community included the A.E.F. States, Madagascar and France.
[26] Constitution du 4 Octobre 1958, Titre XII, Article 82.
[27] Ibid., Article 83.
[28] Ibid., Article 84.

inhabitants than it would to a large federation. Yet a third possibility was offered by de Gaulle, however. So deep-rooted was the paternalist attitude to colonial peoples, that the framers of the Constitution provided for the retention by the 'territoires d'outre-mer' of their status within the French Republic. This would entitle them to become 'soit départements d'Outre-Mer de la République, soit, groupés ou non entre eux, Etats membres de la Communauté.'[29]

But, despite the detailed thought given to its elaboration, the Constitution of the Fifth Republic did not contain any juridical description of the political entity it embodied, while Article 88 stated laconically: 'La République ou la Communauté peuvent conclure des accords avec des Etats qui désirent s'associer à elles, pour développer leurs civilisations.' The overseas deputies in the Paris Assembly were dropped, but the overseas territories participated in presidential elections; the French legislative chambers were made responsible for France alone, while the Community's 'Sénat' included French ministers. The French Cabinet would henceforth concern itself solely with domestic matters, but these would include the disbursement of the French taxpayers' money for the benefit of the overseas territories. Furthermore, there would be no need for federal structures centred on Dakar and Brazzaville except in so far as the autonomous Territories might enter into associations of their own.

In July 1958, de Gaulle's Government had enabled the African Vice-Presidents of the 'Conseils de Gouvernement' to become Prime Ministers presiding over their own Cabinets instead of the Governors. When the draft Constitution was released in August, de Gaulle toured Africa from Madagascar to Senegal. Everywhere, except in Guinea and Niger, the proposals met with an enthusiastic

[29] Constitution du 4 Octobre 1958, Titre XI, Article 76. For a clear and dispassionate analysis of the Fifth Republic's Constitution, see Maurice Duverger, *La cinquième république* (Paris, Presses Universitaires de France, 1959) especially pp. 23–230.

welcome. The clause containing the option of independence was added after discussions with the Abbé Youlou and Senghor in Brazzaville. Thereafter, all the Territories' leaders, except Sékou Touré and Niger's Djiko Bakary, urged their peoples to vote 'oui' in the Referendum.

The Referendum of 28 September 1958 precipitated a crisis between the Guinea, Soudan and Ivory Coast branches of the R.D.A. over the two issues on which it was fundamentally divided, African unity and independence.

Sékou Touré and his half-brother Ismail, head of the powerful neo-Communist group within the P.D.G., already restless under Houphouët-Boigny's conservative and franco-phile leadership, determined to take the opportunity offered by the Referendum to achieve immediate independence. Sékou Touré's speeches during the summer of 1958 display a crescendo of irritation and impatience with de Gaulle's projects. He contemptuously dismissed them as 'l'Union Française rebaptisée, c'est-à-dire la vieille marchandise dont on a changé l'étiquette'.[30] The meeting between Touré and de Gaulle, in Conakry on 25 August had done nothing to calm the former's thoughts or feelings. It was during his famous public speech, in the General's presence, that Touré uttered the words: 'Nous préférons la pauvreté dans la liberté à la richesse dans l'esclavage'.[31] This so appalled de Gaulle that, sensing what the result of the forthcoming Referendum would be, he told his entourage and the Governor: 'Eh bien, messieurs, voilà un homme avec lequel nous ne nous entendrons jamais. Allons, la chose est claire: nous partirons le 29 au matin.'[32]

Sékou Touré hoped that independence would be achieved in association with other A.O.F. Territories. If not, Guinea was prepared to isolate herself provisionally

[30] Sékou Touré, *Expérience guinéenne et unité africaine* (Paris, Présence Africaine, 1961) p. 190.
[31] Jean Lacouture, p. 350.
[32] Ibid., p. 352. See also Lacouture's 'Le dialogue de Conakry' in *Le Monde Hebdomadaire*, 21–27 August 1958.

from the other Territories and to form the first cell of a new type of union based on partial or total abandonment of sovereignty, with the wider object of cementing African unity. Economic considerations doubtless strengthened Touré's resolve, for Guinea, already exporting iron and bauxite, could rely on dollars to finance the Konkouré hydro-electric scheme.

The 'Union Soudanaise' asserted that the independence it desired must be achieved by the African territories collectively and that the R.D.A. should on no account be split. For Soudan's leader, Modibo Keïta, Mayor of Bamako and last President of the A.O.F.'s 'Grand Conseil', was not as yet in complete political control of the territory and had to take into account the policy of Senegal, through which most of Soudan's external trade passed. For tactical reasons only Keïta agreed with Houphouët-Boigny, whose protégé he had been, on the advisability of remaining within the Community, while disagreeing that this could be an end in itself. A man with federalist ambitions, he had twice visited Accra and had been won over to Nkrumah's Pan-Africanism. Houphouët-Boigny, representing the Ivory Coast, had himself virtually drawn up the clauses of the Constitution pertaining to the Community.

The Referendum appeared to represent an impressive victory for de Gaulle. The vote in all the territories except Niger, where despite the opposition of the local leadership under Bakary there was a 78 per cent 'yes' vote, followed the views of the party leaders. Thus, in Guinea 97 per cent of the electorate voted against the Constitution and in the Ivory Coast 99 per cent voted for it. It seems probable, as Professor Carrington has suggested, that in those two States, which had large 'resemblances and the same economic and cultural relations with metropolitan France' this was a vote of confidence in the respective political leaders 'who had succeeded in organising the electorates of their countries and had committed them to political programmes which were only half understood'.[33]

The older élites lost little time in consolidating their victory. In Niger, Bakary and his Cabinet were forced to resign and were replaced by a Government headed by the R.D.A. leader, Hamani Diori, who had held office from 1956 to 1957 as a radical labour organiser with sufficient political intuition to move to the right when Houphouët-Boigny abandoned his Communist connexion. Elections were held in Niger in December 1958 and the R.D.A. registered a sweeping victory, gaining forty-nine out of the sixty seats. Bakary's Socialists—now known as the Sawaba (Freedom) Party—fell from forty to five seats.

By its decision to vote against the Constitution, Guinea cut herself off from the seven A.O.F. States which chose to remain within the Community. Meeting after the Referendum, the R.D.A. voted to expel Touré and his Guinea 'section', while Houphouët-Boigny emphasised his interpretation of the Community as a permanent institution with separate political units.[34] But Senghor went out of his way to state that it was merely a milestone on the road to independence, on the pattern of British dependencies;[35] Sérou Apithy, Prime Minister of Dahomey, said that he would work for the economic and social development which would enable Dahomey to become an independent state.[36] Thus, although the older élites maintained their primacy, they did so only by adopting the shibboleths of African nationalism.

Part 4 Fall of the Community

The Community proved to be very short-lived. Even the most sceptical of observers could not have foretold that by

[33] C. E. Carrington 'Decolonization: the Last Stages' in *International Affairs*, vol. 38, no. 1, January 1962, p. 34.
[34] Cf. *Le Monde*, 12–13 October, 1958.
[35] Cf. *Le Monde*, 2 October 1958.
[36] Ibid.

the summer of 1960 the structure so painstakingly set up by de Gaulle only two years earlier would no longer exist. The struggle in Algeria was one of the factors which contributed to the break-up, but Nkrumah's Pan-Africanism proved even more explosive. Nkrumah's personality does nothing to encourage calm appraisal. To Richard Wright, the American Negro writer, Nkrumah appeared as early as 1955 to be 'l'agent provocateur des émotions de millions d'indigènes'.[37] To the young Dahomeyan writer, Albert Tevoedjre, he merits unstinted praise for having fashioned Ghana, 'L'étoile et la cellule première des Etats-Unis d'Afrique'.[38] More recently, and no doubt more judiciously, Barbara Ward has written that 'Dr. Nkrumah may not be accepted as a leader of continental scope. But few African statesmen can ignore the influence of his passionate Pan-Africanism, especially among the younger men'.[39]

In French-speaking Africa, Nkrumah had already deeply influenced leaders such as Sékou Touré, Saifoulaye Diallo (who negotiated Guinea's 1959 Russian loan and is her number two politician) and Modibo Keïta. Under the influence of George Padmore[40] Nkrumah gave Pan-Africanism a new and powerful twist. Until the fifties 'back-to-Africa' had been its central theme; this was now succeeded by emphasis on the emancipation of colonial territories and their amalgamation into a large state. In the course of the second of the Pan-African conferences to be held on African soil, at which there were 250 delegates from twenty-eight nations, resolutions were passed attacking 'the reactionary character of the institution of the chieftaincy and its sordid support for colonialism', and characterising as 'territories where indigenous Africans are dominated by

[37] Richard Wright, *Puissance noire* (Paris, 1955).
[38] Albert Tevoedjre, p. 41.
[39] Barbara Ward Jackson, 'Free Africa and the Common Market' in *Foreign Affairs*, vol. 40, no. 3, April 1962, pp. 419-420.
[40] George Padmore, a West Indian born in Trinidad, was a leading figure in the Pan-African movement. From 1947 until his death in 1959 he served as Nkrumah's adviser on African affairs.

foreigners' the then already autonomous republics of French-speaking Africa as well as Sierra Leone and Nigeria. This attack came as a complete surprise and shock to most of the French-African delegates who, with the exception of the Guineans, had all been kept isolated throughout the conference. The conference also condemned the use of African soldiers 'in a nefarious global game against their brethren' in Cameroun, where an insurrection had broken out against a lawfully constituted African Government, and in the Ivory Coast, where riots between local inhabitants and immigrants from Dahomey had been quelled by Houphouët-Boigny's security force.

Almost all African leaders believe that their recently independent states should co-operate in economic, cultural, educational and public health matters. The first attempt at association, the Ghana-Guinea-Mali Union, has however proved immature and ill-conceived. On the political plane each African leader of any consequence has his own ideas concerning the type of association and who should lead it. The four most enthusiastic champions of political association are Nkrumah, Touré, Keïta and Azikiwe of Nigeria. Nkrumah has gone so far as to amend the constitution of Ghana in such a way as to give the legislature the power to surrender 'the whole or any part of the sovereignty of Ghana' to facilitate the creation of a union of African states. The Pan-African ideas which have become an intrinsic part of the ideologies of Guinea and Mali have been expressed in a more moderate form by Senghor, who thinks in terms of a 'regroupement' of the French-speaking states and who prefers to stress the cultural value of 'négritude' rather than the more fundamental realities of Pan-Africanism. The latter however have a strong popular appeal in the poorer States of Niger, Upper Volta and Dahomey.

A third contributory factor to the rapid disintegration of the Community was the stimulation of centrifugal forces by the independence of Ghana and Guinea and by recent events in Togo and Cameroun. In 1958 Togo and

Cameroun were still French trust territories under the United Nations, whose evolution had influenced developments in the two French-speaking federations both before and after the 'loi cadre'. Immediately after the Referendum Togo and Cameroun sought to bring France's trusteeship to an end. Sylvanus Olympio, Prime Minister of Togo, and Ahmadou Ahidjo, Prime Minister of Cameroun, flew to Paris in October 1958 to negotiate their territories' independence. By 1960 their trusteeship status had been discarded. Olympio has since expressed the hope that the Ghana-Guinea Union may be expanded to embrace other West African states, such as Togo. Ahidjo on the other hand is fearful of the attraction of Ghana; he brought about the federation of Cameroun with the smaller Southern Cameroons on 1 October 1961.

Thus the community was but an ephemeral organisation, useful because it bridged the transition from colonial status to independence, but condemned to failure because it was not sufficiently resilient to resist the counter-attraction of former British and French possessions. De Gaulle continued to offset statements that the African Territories could leave the Community at any time by explicit denials that it would ever be allowed to develop into a French version of the British Commonwealth.

By 1960, however, French resistance to the principle of African independence was finally overcome. On 4 June the French Government sponsored an amendment to the 1958 Constitution's Titre XII, enabling any State to be sovereign and yet remain within what has come to be called the 'Communauté rénovée'. When it became clear that independence could be achieved without such deprivation of economic aid as Guinea had suffered, all the autonomous republics chose independence. In Paris it had been hoped that this gesture would safeguard at least the façade, if not the substance, of the Community. But instead of taking on the aspect of a 'Commonwealth à la française',[41] the 'Communauté' simply collapsed. Only a few states—Senegal, the four former A.E.F. States and Madagascar—adhered to the 'Communauté rénoveé'.

Meanwhile, the convinced federalists in both the inter-territorial parties, the R.D.A. and P.R.A., had decided to reconstitute a federal system. Modibo Keïta joined forces with Senghor, Guèye and Dia. He devoted his energies to the task of creating the Federation of Mali, originally designed to comprise Senegal, Soudan, Dahomey and Upper Volta, whose representatives agreed at their meeting at Bamako in December 1958 to establish a new French-speaking West African Federation. A provisional constitution, with the motto 'Un Peuple, un But, une Foi', was approved at Dakar in January 1959. But a combination of pressures from France, from the Ivory Coast and from within, compelled the Governments of Dahomey and Upper Volta to withdraw.

When the Federation of Mali came into being, in April 1959, it comprised only Senegal and Soudan, with Senghor as President of its 'Assemblée Nationale' and Keïta as Prime Minister. By June 1960, Mali (described by Senghor as 'une nation négro-africaine de l'occident',)[42] was recognised as a sovereign State and continued to co-operate with France and the other members of the Community. But the Federation, based on what proved to be but a temporary association of two distinct parties—the 'Union Progressiste Sénégalaise' and the 'Union Soudanaise'—very soon broke up in an undignified manner. The tensions which drove a wedge between the two parties and led to the Federation's disruption in August 1960 appeared to relate to the distribution of offices and patronage within the new State. In actual fact, as is now appreciated, the antagonism was more

[41] Cf. Léopold Sédar Senghor, *African Socialism* (New York, American Society of African Culture, 1959), p. 9.
[42] Cf. Congrès Constitutif du P.R.A.: *Rapport sur la Doctrine et le Programme du Parti* (Paris, Présence Africaine, 1959) p. 87.

deep-rooted and was caused by the incompatibility of the two parties' political philosophies—the conflict between gradualism and radicalism in economic and social policy and between a francophile and a markedly Pan-African orientation. Added to these were differences in their theories of the State. After the split, Soudan retained the name 'Mali'. The new Republic of Mali aligned itself with the Accra-Conakry axis, while at a meeting in Conakry in December 1960 Nkrumah, Touré and Keïta agreed to form the Ghana-Guinea-Mali Union, whose proclaimed object was to 'harmonise and co-ordinate the policies of the three states' in all spheres.[43]

Of quite a different type was the federal union created by Houphouët-Boigny. Mindful of the existence of strong federalist elements in Volta, Niger and Dahomey, of which Mali might take advantage in order to offset the loss of Senegal, Houphouët-Boigny buried his objections to political federations and led one himself. He pointed out to Maurice Yaméogo, Volta's Prime Minister, that the latter's country was linked to the Ivory Coast by the Abidjan-Ouagadougou railway, while no adequate communications existed between Volta and the Federation of Mali or Dahomey, which were its only other outlets to the sea. To the Moro Naba, Emperor of Volta's Mossi tribesmen, Houphouët-Boigny—in his capacity as a tribal chieftain—artfully stressed the powerlessness to which Senegal and Soudan had reduced their traditional chiefs.

In Dahomey, Apithy had never been an enthusiastic advocate of federation with Senegal and Soudan, since Niger refused to consider the project. He resigned from the 'Parti de la Fédération Africaine',[44] stating that he could not support the Federation of Mali at the expense of Dahomey's free growth and economy. This was explicit

[43] Hodgkin and Schachter, p. 426.
[44] Formed in March 1959, as a new inter-territorial party, based on the U.P.S. and the 'Union Soudanaise', with 'sections' in Dahomey, Volta and Niger.

recognition of the fact that Dahomey's prosperity is geared to its role as a maritime outlet for Niger and Volta's eastern region.

Niger is the largest of the former A.O.F. Territories but, being mostly desert, is very thinly inhabited and suffers from severe shortage of water. The only city of importance is Niamey which has developed considerably since 1945. Domestic slavery is practised by the nomadic chiefs who elude government control. Niger is formally independent but is quite incapable of standing on its own. Its Premier Hamani Diori welcomes any aid that he can obtain from the Ivory Coast, Dahomey and Volta.

The 'Sahel-Bénin Union' was a much looser form of association than the Mali Federation. It was dominated by the Ivory Coast, the wealthiest of the four republics and the only one under the effective control of a mass party. Its form reflected the views of the P.D.C.I. and of Houphouët-Boigny, whom Yaméogo described as 'notre Général à nous'. Although there was to be no federal capital and assembly, since Houphouët-Boigny maintained that Africa could not afford a multiplicity of institutions, a 'Conseil de l'Entente' was set up composed of the prime ministers and of representatives of the four Republics' 'Assemblées'. At its first meeting in May 1959 the 'Conseil' agreed to co-ordinate policies on justice, finance, the civil service, labour, communications and public health. A customs union was established and a 'Fonds de Solidarité'. This fund was financed from contributions equivalent to 10 per cent of the revenues of each State and could be used for floating international loans for development purposes. It was divided as follows: each of the other three Republics received five-sixteenths, the Ivory Coast one-sixteenth. Since the Ivory Coast received only one-fifth of the amount allocated to each of the other Republics, while contributing on average four dollars to every one of theirs, Houphouët-Boigny may be said to have agreed to contribute to the support and development of the other three associates on a permanent basis. Such a commitment constituted a complete reversal of his previous attitude to federalism and its economic implications. His role as the A.O.F.'s foremost 'particularist' leader from 1956 onwards had been prompted by his country's profound sense of economic grievance: its belief that it was the A.O.F.'s milch-cow, the A.O.F.'s Katanga. Under French rule, rebates and subsidies from the Federal Government made up 35 to 50 per cent of the total territorial government income of the richer territories such as the Ivory Coast and Senegal, and as much as 90 per cent of the territorial government income of such poor territories as Niger.[45] The Ivory Coast's large contribution to the A.O.F.'s federal budget accounts for Houphouët-Boigny's persistent refusal to countenance any new federation between 1956 and 1959, when the first draft of the Mali Federation threatened to entrench the principle of Pan-Africanism in French-speaking West Africa with such strategic skill as to render it virtually inexpugnable. Thus the Mali Entente dichotomy proved to be a 1959 version, in a more acute form, of the earlier polar opposition between Dakar and Abidjan.

In May 1959, the 'Entente' leaders accepted Houphouët-Boigny's interpretation of the Community. But after December 1959, when General de Gaulle agreed that Mali could obtain independence and yet remain within the Community,[46] this interpretation was no longer tenable. Thereafter, the 'Entente' States were bound to demand independence if their status in the Community was to remain equal to that of Mali. Very reluctantly and with pardonable ill-grace, Houphouët-Boigny agreed that their demands be tabled in June 1960. The demands were for immediate independence in August and French sponsorship for admission to the United Nations as a precondition to

[45] Cf. Elliot J. Berg, 'The Economic Basis of Political Choice in French West Africa' in *The American Political Science Review*, vol. LIV, no. 2, June 1960, pp. 391–405.
[46] Cf. *Notes et Etudes Documentaires No. 2,739*, 13 January 1961, p. 12.

negotiating special defence, economic aid and cultural
agreements with France.

What policies would the new sovereign States pursue?
What would their relations with France be; would they
seek to reconstitute a wider association than the 'Communauté rénovée', on equal terms with France; or would
they form several associations, each bearing a hallmark that
would identify them with some aspect of Pan-Africanism?
The events which swiftly followed upon the granting of
independence were proof of the fact that regional groupings
were taking place among all the French-speaking African
States. From the time of admission to the United Nations
in September 1960[47] the political leaders met frequently to
discuss international problems, while Houphouët-Boigny,
Senghor, Dia and Olympio worked to form an association of
their states. Houphouët-Boigny, while skilfully pointing the
moral of the Mali Federation's failure, stressed his theory
that any such association should be flexible. His adjurations
did not fall on deaf ears, so far as Senghor and Dia were
concerned. These two were still extremely resentful of their
treatment at the hands of Modibo Keïta, and expressed
open approval of the structure of the 'Conseil de l'Entente'.
By September 1960, most observers believed that a formal
reconciliation, demonstrated by political agreement, would
take place between Dakar and Abidjan.

Part 5   The Brazzaville Bloc

The moderate African political leaders agreed to convene
a series of conferences to be attended by representatives of
the French-speaking States.[48] These conferences were
intended to take the place of the meetings of the 'Conseil
Exécutif', abolished at the break-up of the Community.
There is little doubt that they were impelled to take these

---

[47] Except Mauritania, whose admission was blocked by the Soviet Union.
[48] The Conferences were held as follows: Abidjan (October 1960);
Nouakchott (November 1960); Brazzaville (December 1960); Dakar
(January-February 1961); Yaoundé (March 1961); Tananarive
(September 1961).

steps in view of France's apparent unconcern about events in tropical Africa. De Gaulle was by then more deeply involved than ever in the intricacies of the Algerian situation and had begun to display greater interest in NATO and his own new theory of 'l'Europe des patries', than in Africa south of the Sahara. At the Conference of Yaoundé in March 1961 the African states known as the 'Groupe de Brazzaville'[49]—that is to say the four 'Entente' States, the four Republics of the former A.E.F.[50], Senegal, Mauritania, Cameroun and Madagascar—agreed to form the 'Union Africaine et Malgache'. This was a new type of 'Community' of African states, without the participation of France. France had, however, already signed special agreements with all her former territories in tropical Africa except Guinea. This Union, unlike that of the rival bloc formed by Ghana, Guinea and Mali, does not claim to be anything but an organisation for co-operation in political and diplomatic matters with its own administration. An 'Organisation Africaine et Malgache de Coopération Economique' was set up for the co-ordination of internal and external trade policies, customs tariffs, currency and industrial projects. The members' Development Plans are to be examined by the Organisation, headed by a Cameroun General Secretary and located at Yaoundé.

Two hostile blocs have thus been formed in French West Africa. On the one hand there are the Brazzaville States, whose élite are steeped in French culture—the 'métissage intellectuel' to which Senghor has often referred. Led by able and energetic, though moderate, men, who have become Presidents of their respective Republics, they are friendly to the West. And on the other hand, a bloc of 'revolutionary' states (three of which—Guinea, Mali, Morocco—are French-speaking) centred on Accra and

[49] So called because, at the Conference at Brazzaville in December 1960, they decided to constitute a bloc of French-speaking States.
[50] They had formed the 'Union des Républiques de l'Afrique Equatoriale', primarily an economic and customs union, in 1960.

dedicated to Pan-Africanism. This bloc merges into the wider 'Casablanca' group of states, and acts as a leaven within that group. The rift between the two blocs has widened as a result of the Monrovia and Lagos Conferences, and the Casablanca group's refusal to attend.

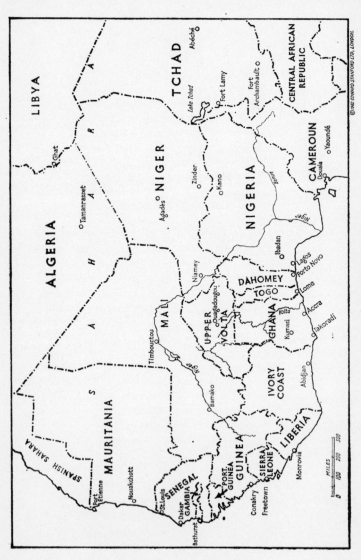

French-Speaking West Africa since 1959

VI THE FUTURE

BUT what of the future of French-speaking Africa? Two main trends emerge. Although political relations between these African states and France are of diminishing importance because of the increasing significance of inter-African relations, patterns of trade and the need for financial and economic assistance link French-speaking Africa more closely to the West than to the Soviet bloc and, what is more, more closely to France than to any other Western State. For, despite the movement of thought in France known as 'cartierisme',[1] which claims that French investments in Africa can never again prove profitable, France spent £251 million in aid to Africa, in 1960, as against Britain's £48 million, the United States' £77 million and the Soviet Union's £95 million. The scepticism in certain circles in France is based on the fear that French assets in the African states may be nationalised, as has happened in Guinea, where the most recent cases have been the last remaining privately-owned bank, the Banque de l'Afrique Occidentale, which was closed down in January 1962, and the Bauxites du Midi (a subsidiary of Aluminium Ltd., which had some $23 million invested in Guinea) whose property was taken over, by presidential decree, in February. The F.R.I.A. may prove equally vulnerable. The 'cartieristes' and others also point to the luxury and extravagance that characterise the life of many West Africans in responsible office.

But the French-speaking African states are not likely to relinquish the great advantages derived—except by Guinea —from their status of Associated Overseas Territories of the European Economic Community. This status, guaranteed under the Treaty of Rome, is due solely to the good offices of France. In addition, these States have been able to enter

[1] From a series of articles by Raymond Cartier in the popular weekly, *Paris-Match*.

into extremely valuable bilateral agreements with France. That signed between the Ivory Coast and France, in April 1961, may be taken as an example. In return for favourable conditions on the French market for its coffee and bananas, the Ivory Coast granted France privileged outlets for products whose market is organised within the framework of the franc zone, e.g. sugar, cereals and edible oils, and for certain other products, reviewed annually. In addition, the Ivory Coast was granted unrestricted access to the franc zone's foreign exchange market.[2] The value of such special agreements between France and its former African colonies (including Mali which, though associated with Ghana and Guinea, has remained in the franc zone and signed a series of agreements of co-operation with France early in February 1962) is all the more obvious when studied in the light of conditions in Guinea. The Guinean franc continues to decline and it is reported that the currency, whose official rate is 691 to the pound, is being exchanged in Freetown at about 1,500 and in Abidjan at up to 2,000 to the pound. Consumer goods are in short supply in Guinea and the country's balance of payments is in heavy imbalance. Sékou Touré and his countrymen now realise that the Communist countries desire payment for their aid and credits.

Because the policy of political assimilation had its economic counterpart in an inclusive system of economic relations between France and its overseas possessions, France's African colonies—unlike the former British West African dependencies which were taught to pay their way—could not stand on their own feet economically upon achieving independence. The close economic links with France had to be maintained as a matter of 'force majeure'. This has resulted in a political, as well as an economic, polarisation towards France and hence towards the West.

[2] Cf. Three-Monthly Economic Review, *Former French Tropical Africa and Liberia* (London, The Economist Intelligence Unit) no. 8, February 1962, pp. 2–3.

Since their leaders are moderate men with a keener interest in developing their country than in embracing or fashioning ideologies, the French-speaking States may act as a stabilising influence in Africa. A new scramble for Africa has begun. This time it is not to carve up territories, but to forestall other powers in lending money and thus winning influence though it will be of little use to the newly independent states of Africa unless it enables them to develop balanced economies which clearly should be related to their natural wealth, their labour potential, their geographical and climatic conditions. Well-planned aid is all the more essential, since the gap between the developed and the underdeveloped peoples in material well-being and technological skill continues to widen.

The second major trend is toward autocratic government. Though the type of political system or systems which will emerge among the new States of Africa is still undefined, it is doubtful whether the majority of Africans regard the Western pattern of parliamentary democracy with any real respect. The normal processes of political democracy were but seldom genuinely applied in the former dependencies in the days of colonial rule. Certainly not very often in the French colonies where, after the Second World War and at a period when it was surely essential to instruct Africans as fully as possible in the difficult task of democratic government based on representative institutions, numerous examples of dishonest manipulation of the democratic process have been noted. Such cases did not pass unobserved by the Africans against whom the frauds were perpetrated.

As Chief H. O. Davies of Nigeria has recently stated, 'the ordinary people do not understand party politics, except as a call to war against the members of the rival parties. The martial spirit in the people, which had become moribund or latent with the abolition of the slave trade and the stoppage of raiding expeditions, seems to be suddenly aroused by the coming of politics.'[3] Lord Balfour wrote in 1927: 'Constitutions are easily copied, temperaments are not; and if it should happen that the borrowed constitution and the native temperament fail to correspond, the misfit may have serious results'.[4] He went on to describe the essence of a true parliamentary democracy's political machinery when he stated that it presupposed 'a people so fundamentally at one that they can afford to bicker'.[5] More recently, in the lectures which he delivered at the Sorbonne when Ambassador to Paris, K. M. Panikkar warned his audience that it must expect representative forms of government to suffer setbacks, when introduced into countries in which the system's implications are not fully understood by the leaders themselves.[6]

And so, all that may be said at this juncture is that Western democracy is not going to work in Africa—with the possible exception of Nigeria, which, like India, is buttressed by a strong federal structure and has an effective Opposition. Though it may well, at its worst, degenerate into a mere 'communauté de convoitises', within a tribal framework, the average independent African State is more likely to produce something new in political organisation, a symbiosis that may well utilise the form, though not the substance, of democracy. It will no doubt continue to draw inspiration and strength from its single-party structure, but only so long as creative impulses are permitted to reach the apex of the monolith from the lower levels of the party hierarchy, while also percolating downwards from the apex.[7] As it is, the *parti unique* is now in complete control throughout the area I

[3] H. O. Davies, 'The New African Profile', in *Foreign Affairs*, vol. 40 no. 2, January 1962, p. 295.
[4] Preface to Walter Bagehot's *The English Constitution* (The World's Classics Edition, 1936) p. xxii.
[5] Ibid., p. xxiv.
[6] Cf. K. M. Panikkar, *The Afro-Asian States and Their Problems* (London, George Allen & Unwin, 1959) especially pp. 15–30.
[7] Cf. Franz Ansprenger, *Politik im Schwarzen Afrika*; *Die modernen politischen Bewegungen im Afrika französischer Prägung* (Cologne, West-deutscher Verlag, 1961) p. 424.

have been discussing. There are members of opposition parties (which have all been either disbanded, outlawed or disqualified from contesting elections[8]) who are in prison in Senegal and the Ivory Coast as well as in Guinea and Mali and the former A.O.F. territories.[9] No doubt French-speaking Africa will develop on its own lines and may find a philosopher who will give it new intellectual expression, for neither Marxism nor Gandhiism is likely to prove a satisfactory substitute for the prophets of liberal democracy who have been so emphatically rejected by the African states.

Class structures in Africa are ill-defined and there is virtually no 'class struggle' as known to Marxists. Madeira Keïta, Mali's Minister of the Interior, was able to instance this in his justification of the existence of the *parti unique* in present-day Africa when he declared:

Je dis que l'Afrique ne doit pas se battre sur le terrain de l'idéologie tel qu'elle est comprise par l'Occident, car nous n'avons pas de problèmes religieux ou philosophiques qui nous divisent pour l'administration de la cité; nous n'avons pas de problèmes religieux, de problèmes philosophiques ou de problèmes de théorie économique qui nous divisent pour la construction et la direction de l'Etat.[10]

---

[8] Cf. Hodgkin, *African Political Parties*, pp. 179–209.
[9] Eve Dessarre, *Quel sera le destin de l'Afrique?* (Paris, Plon, 1961) pp. 38–78.
[10] Madeira Keïta, 'Le parti unique en Afrique' in *Présence Africaine* (Paris, février-mars 1960) p. 14.

Printed in Great Britain by
R. J. Acford Ltd.,
Chichester, Sussex